WOLF'S LAIR

WOLF'S LAIR

INSIDE HITLER'S EAST PRUSSIAN HQ

IAN BAXTER

'Men and wars come and go, but what is left, are the buildings.'

Adolf Hitler

First published 2009

The History Press
The Mill, Brimscombe Port
Stroud, Gloucestershire, GL5 2QG
www.thehistorypress.co.uk

British Library Cataloguing in Publication Data.
A catalogue record for this book is available from the British Library.

ISBN 978 0 7509 5079 4

Printed in Great Britain

Contents

Pamphlet

About the Author

Ian Baxter is a military historian who specialises in German twentieth-century military history. He has written more than twenty books including *Poland – The Eighteen Day Victory March, Panzers In North Africa, The Ardennes Offensive, The Western Campaign, The 12th SS Panzer-Division Hitlerjugend, The Waffen-SS on the Western Front, The Waffen-SS on the Eastern Front, The Red Army At Stalingrad, Elite German Forces of World War II, Armoured Warfare, German Tanks of War, Blitzkrieg, Panzer-Divisions At War, Hitler's Panzers, German Armoured Vehicles of World War Two, Last Two Years of the Waffen-SS At War, German Soldier Uniforms and Insignia, German Guns of the Third Reich, Defeat to Retreat: The Last Years of the German Army At War 1944–1945, Operation Bagration – the destruction of Army Group Centre, German Guns of the Third Reich, Rommel and the Afrika Korps, U-Boat War,* and most recently *The Sixth Army and the Road to Stalingrad. The SS of Treblinka* is a forthcoming History Press title. He has written over one hundred journal articles including 'Last days of Hitler', 'Wolf's Lair', 'Story of the V1 and V2 rocket programme', 'Secret Aircraft of World War Two', 'Rommel at Tobruk', 'Hitler's War with his Generals', 'Secret British Plans to Assassinate Hitler', 'SS at Arnhem', 'Hitlerjugend, Battle Of Caen 1944', 'Gebirgsjäger at War', 'Panzer Crews', 'Hitlerjugend Guerrillas', 'Last Battles in the East', 'Battle of Berlin', and many more. He has also reviewed numerous military studies for publication, supplied thousands of photographs and important documents to various publishers and film production companies worldwide, and lectures to various schools, colleges and universities throughout the United Kingdom and Ireland.

Acknowledgements

Those of us who write the histories of war know what an arduous task it is to put them together, and without help this project would have been impossible. So I will endeavour to first thank those who shared my research, to briefly name the historians and archivists who guided me, and the friends whose help went beyond the bounds of professional assistance. I first wish to thank my Polish expert and translator Bartlomiej Zoborski. He not only found vital contacts, but revealed valuable information that became an asset in completing my research.

During my ten years of research into Hitler's headquarters, I must also acknowledge David Irving for his help and expert advice. A special debt is due to Dr Hans-Jurgen Kuhn, Professor Peter Hoffmann of McGill University, Montreal, Canada, whose advice and book, *Hitler's Personal Security*, helped me throughout my research. I wish to thank Dr Andrzei Paczkowski, Fritz T. Stol, and of course Dr Richard Raiber of Hockessin, Delaware, USA, whose diligent and expert advice clarified many issues and diverse opinions.

Thanks also go to Linda Mcfeddon, my German historical diary translator for deciphering many illegible handwritten diaries. As ever, I am much in debt to the staff of the Imperial War Museum in London, archivist Robin Edward Cookson for captured German records at the National Archives USA, Ulrike Talay and Michael Volk at the *Intitut fur Zeigeschichte Archiv Munchen*, Bundesarchiv Koblenz, and Dr Ritter at the *Bundesarchiv Berlin*, for their help, advice, access to documents and other important information.

My thanks go to Mr Boguslaw Wrobel of 'EXPLORATOR' in Poland, Michelle Mortimer who was Publishing Manager at the MicroForm in West Yorkshire, England, Professor Dr Hartmut Lehmann of the *Max-Planck-*

Institut Für Geschichte (since 2007 the *Max-Planck-Institut zur Erforschung multireligiöser und multiethnischer Gesellschaften*), The German Historical Institute in London and the staff at the Colchester Library in England.

I must especially record my appreciation of the kindness of the staff at the Ilford Park residential home in Devon, England, and to W. Jaworski who generously gave his time to translate Polish and Russian documents for me.

To many individuals I owe thanks for their help, personal reminiscence and unfailing encouragement. I have spoken briefly of all those who had some association with my research on this book, but not yet those that actually ventured with me to Poland to see the ruins of the Wolf's Lair. It is with the greatest pleasure that I would like to thank my dear friends Kevin Bowden and Chandran Sivaneson for coming to Poland with me over a three-day period. It was a cold and snowy morning in January 2008 when we arrived in Gdansk airport. Our Polish guide and taxi driver, Elzbieta Giste, took us across northern Poland, and after travelling more than five hours across treacherous roads to the east of the country, we finally arrived safely in the town of Ketzryn (formerly Rastenburg) to begin our research into Hitler's infamous East Prussian headquarters. To both Kevin and Chandran I would like to say a big thank you. Not only were they extremely helpful with their support and advice but they were infinitely patient as they waited for me in the snow, examining each ruined building. My gratitude also goes to Elzbieta Giste who helped us tirelessly with translation and driving us around the Polish countryside.

Preface

This is the special and wonderful property of architecture: when the work has been done, a monument remains. That endures; it is something different from a pair of boots, which can also be made, but which the wearer wears out in a year or two and then throws away. This remains, and through the centuries will bear witness to all those who helped to create it.

Adolf Hitler, following the construction of the Reich Chancellery in January 1939.

I held this ardent belief when I embarked on this study of Hitler's largest wartime headquarters, the Wolf's Lair. Throughout my years of research I saw myself not as an architect concerned with building towering structures, but an historian eager to construct in words a lasting monument to Hitler's Eastern Front headquarters.

The Wolf's Lair (*Wolfschanze*) was the most important German command post built during the Second World War, and the orders that were sent from these secret headquarters inevitably changed the course of the War. Still to this day, many people persistently cloak these headquarters in an atmosphere of gloom to reinforce the image of the frightening Führer who lived there. However, it is my opinion that the legacy left by Hitler at his headquarters is self-evident and requires no exaggerated portrayal. In order to remedy this unnecessary obfuscation I decided to burrow deep and describe events from behind the barbed-wire entanglements of the Wolf's Lair and analyse each unfolding episode through the eyes of Hitler and his staff.

In writing this study of one of the most interesting military headquarters of the twentieth century, I found the results of my research astonishing, for there was no single comprehensive document which I could consult.

I therefore approached the research as a giant puzzle. In order to piece it together I sought not only the printed text of military books, unpublished records, documents, archives, and the advice of military experts in the field, but I dug deep into the contemporary writings of his closest personal staff, seeking to disentangle the truth through letters written by wives, friends, adjutants, private secretaries, physicians, and of course his military staff. I waded through many hundreds of pages of microfilm, scrutinizing information on those that lived and worked at the headquarters. I even went further by advertising in the *Gazeta* – a Polish national newspaper – appealing for persons that had worked constructing the headquarters site, and at the same time, in Germany, advertised in the paper, *Der Freiwillige*.

I am aware that some readers may find such a study far from complete, or may even take it as granting a kind of undue recognition to a number of people described in it. But we must know about the motives of those that were present when the momentous decisions were taken if we are to understand those decisions.

The purpose of this volume is to examine life within the *Führerhauptquartiere* (Führer's headquarters), where, from behind closed doors inside the wooden hutments and the claustrophobic atmosphere of bunkers, Hitler planned and gossiped with his associates. He was regularly seen taking strolls around the perimeter of what was known as his 'inner sanctum', Security Zone I, even stopping to chat familiarly with the *Organization Todt* workmen that were labouring night and day, building and re-strengthening the many dozens of bunkers and buildings that made up the Wolf's Lair. As setbacks rapidly turned into catastrophe, Hitler surrounded himself not with his intimate circle of friends, but what he considered were illiterate soldiers. Conversation became confined to the barracks and mess.

Consequently, the pages of this text investigate the manner in which Hitler's contempt for his war staff grew. It describes how, during the onset of the traumatic German military reverses in Russia, Hitler stood unbowed in the face of the enemy, and how he tried to infuse determination into his generals and friends, despite his rapid deterioration in health.

Chapter I

Historical Background

The Führer's headquarters or *Führerhauptquartiere* – officially abbreviated FHQu – were the various command posts from which the supreme commander directed military operations during the Second World War. They ranged widely from the rather simple array of railway coaches, nicknamed the *Führersonderzug* (Führer's special train), to an extensive, reinforced, heavily guarded concrete complex called the Wolf's Lair or *Wolfschanze*, built deep in the countryside of East Prussia.

From the very beginning, it is necessary to note that the *Führerhauptquartiere* never bore any relationship to the General Headquarters or *Obersteheersleitung*, the highest German military command centre in the First World War. In 1914 Kaiser Wilhelm II was the commander-in-chief and was expected to take advice from his General Staff of the field army at all times, the German Army's highest general. Generally, the Kaiser interfered very little in military matters, leaving the General Staff to preside over the War, whilst the Kaiser was scarcely more than an invited guest.

Adolf Hitler, however, was certainly no Kaiser Wilhelm II. He had recognized the Kaiser's weakness, and by 4 February 1938 had personally taken command of the armed forces, replaced the War Ministry with the High Command of the armed forces or *Oberkommando der Wehrmacht* (OKW) and acquired for himself the instruments needed for the administration and supply of the armed forces. The chief of the General Staff of the Army no longer functioned as the Army's top general. Instead, he was now an advisor to the Commander-in-Chief of the Army, or what was known as the High Command of the Army or the *Oberkommando des Heeres* (OKH).

Between OKH and Hitler, was the OKW. It was an independent military authority, the nerve centre of the German hierarchy. It was commanded by General Wilhelm Keitel. In Keitel, Hitler had found exactly the type of officer he was seeking. He was someone who would carry out his commands to the letter without question, a 'yes-man' who would be content to receive orders from the Führer without any independent command. With such a responsibility a tremendous workload now rested upon Keitel, and Hitler soon grew accustomed to having this ever conscientious and exceedingly hard-working administrator in charge.

Keitel organized his new command into four sections: the Armed Forces Operations Staff (*Fuhrungstab*/WFA, later *Wehrmacht Fuhrungsstab*/WFSt (Armed Forces Operations Office)), the Intelligence and Counterespionage Office (*Abwehr*, the Armed Forces Central Office), and the Armed Forces Economic Office. The Operations staff was regarded as the most important section, and Keitel chose one of the most suitable military experts for the job, Major-General Alfred Jodl, as Chief of the OKW Operations Office.

The Operations Office, existing alongside OKW, acted as an administrative office for the receipt and processing of reports from the front. It also received orders from Hitler and issued them accordingly. Although both Keitel and Jodl had become part of Hitler's military hierarchy, they actually worked without any real defined responsibilities and command authority. Together, they headed OKW to correlate and supervise individual strategies as conceived and initiated by the three services, the OKH, the *Oberkommando der Marine* (High Command of the Navy), and the *Oberkommando der Luftwaffe* (OKL, the High Command of the Airforce).

Alongside OKW stood the OKH, which was commanded by Colonel-General Walter von Brauchitsch. In Keitel's opinion, he was a gentleman of the old school with sound judgement in military matters who possessed the talent necessary for conducting strategy along classical lines. Brauchitsch's Chief of Staff was Colonel-General Franz Halder, who was the most controversial of all the generals in Hitler's military elite. Halder was a devoted general of the highest competence and his main responsibilities were to form strong planning teams within the General Staff that could challenge the authority of Keitel and Jodl in the OKW.

The first real test of the higher organization of the *Wehrmacht* began with the planned invasion of Poland, code-named 'Case White'. It was here that the new *Führerhauptquartiere* was first established onboard a special train code-named the *Führersonderzug,* the Führer Special. In the days leading to the war, it was not possible to say what made Hitler reject all proposals for the organization of the Army War Headquarters. Though we do know that when Keitel had put forward a semi-complete plan to house it in a newly completed barracks in the Potsdam area of Berlin, Hitler remarked that as supreme commander, he could not move out of Berlin westwards when the Wehrmacht was marching east into Poland. To the public, that would look like deserting his post. So it was that Hitler decided to use his special train as his first headquarters of the war. Only this mobile headquarters could provide the means for him to shuttle back and forth from east to west as the occasion might demand, and more easily visit sectors of the front he was interested in.

On 3 September 1939, Hitler's new mobile headquarters left Berlin's Anhalt station bound for Poland. Among the coaches, there were two baggage and one power-engine cars, the Führer's Pullman, and one press car with a communication centre including a 700-watt short wave transmitter. There was Hitler's extensive guest, dining and personal staff accommodation, including a bathing car. In his personal coach was a drawing room, and attached to these quarters was his communication centre, equipped with radio-telephone and several teletype machines. There was the escort car for the *Reichssicheerheitsdienst* (RSD), Reich Security Service and *Führer-Begleit-Battaillon* (FBB) or Führer Escort Battalion. The remaining coaches consisted of two cars for personnel such as secretaries, cooks, aides, signal corps men, and two sleeping cars for entourage and guests.

In the train, as at the Reich Chancellery, the brown Nazi party uniform dominated the scene. Onboard there were nine or more adjutants and aides, Keitel and Jodl of the OKW (later, each had his own *Sonderzug*), the Führer's army adjutant Gerhard Engel, two personal physicians for the Führer, two secretaries and three or more press officers, including the Reich press chief Otto Dietrich, who was soon to write a short book about the journey. There were several radio operators, guests such as the chief photographer Heinrich Hoffmann, a liaison officer, Heinrich Himmler, Karl Wolff, Martin Bormann's younger brother Albert, a representative of the Foreign Office, three valets, the driver and deputy, ten *SS Begleit-Kommando* men or Führer Escort Battalion (FBB), ten RSD men, fourteen officials and employees of the Reich Railway Catering Service including waiters, cooks, kitchen maids and two silver cleaners, five railway police officers, and three inspectors of the Reich mail. Later, Theodor Eicke also operated his command headquarters for the brutal Death's Head regiments from Hitler's special train.

For the next two weeks, Hitler was to spend most of his waking hours in the claustrophobic atmosphere of his command coach. Here, Keitel introduced the Führer to his Chief of Operations, Alfred Jodl. This tall, balding officer impressed Hitler immediately. Jodl was to be his principal strategic advisor until the end of the War.

From the train Hitler was able to devote his attention entirely to operations in Poland; this was only the first of several journeys the train made. In spite of the advantages in mobility from the very first day it left Berlin for Poland the train had obvious disadvantages as a military headquarters. In fact, on 14 September 1939, in the swaying carriage of the 'command coach', Hitler discussed at length with his chief engineer Fritz Todt the need for a permanent headquarters in the West. Jodl instructed his deputy General Walther Warlimont to reconnoitre for a field headquarters for the OKW to the west of central Germany, from which the later phases of a war against the West could be conducted.

For the next few months, the search was on for the first ground headquarters. As usual, Hitler took up residence in the Chancellery, using it temporarily, as he did throughout the war as supreme headquarters. By April 1940, with the war poised against the West, a new location for the headquarters had been found near the town of Munstereifel, code-named *Felsennest*, Rocky Nest. Hitler had instructed that OKH should be located in a neighbouring hunting lodge, whilst the Luftwaffe chiefs of staff were left to choose their own headquarters.

Hitler's underground command post at *Felsennest* was very small and claustrophobic. But in spite of the gloomy surroundings in which he worked and lived he was able to undertake detailed discussions with his service professionals and execute orders quickly and effectively. From behind the barbed wire entanglements the military leadership were able to plan and order various operations. Commanders fighting on the front lines were influenced daily by the *Führerhauptquartiere*. Many of them were regularly summoned to make a presentation or report, which gave Hitler and his operations staff a more detailed insight into operations being conducted on the frontlines.

For the second phase of the war in the West, Hitler and his headquarters staff moved to the small deserted Belgian village of Bruly-de-Pesche, near the border with France. It was promptly sited in a forest clearing code-named 'Forest Meadow'. However, by the time Hitler arrived on 6 June 1940 he wanted to give these peaceful surroundings a war-like name, *Wolfschlucht* (Wolf's Gorge).

Hitler never felt at home here as he did at *Felsennest*. Whether it was the swarms of mosquitoes that plagued all around or his burning desire to win the war quickly, nobody could tell. Despite his agitation he was supremely confident. The Wehrmacht had achieved rapid success and swept forward almost unimpeded on a 400-mile front, heading for Paris.

When victory had finally been attained during the last week of June OKW and OKH collected themselves from the Wolf's Gorge and surrounding areas and moved deep into the Black Forest in one of the headquarters prepared before the outbreak of the War. Its nickname was *Tannenberg*. Here, Hitler had decided on a short stay before returning to the Chancellery, primarily so that he could visit the great forts of the French Maginot Line. *Tannenberg* was not one of Hitler's most attractively sited headquarters. The tall pine trees swayed with alarming momentum, and it rained heavily for most of his week's stay. When there was sunshine, he could be seen walking through the dripping forest of the restricted part of the headquarters known as HQ Area I, flanked either by guests, party dignitaries or adjutants.

On 6 July, just two months after he had set forth to conquer France, Hitler left the bleak surroundings of *Tannenberg* and boarded his train for Berlin. For the next nine months he spent his time either at the Reich's Chancellery, his mountain retreat in the Berghof, or on board his train, now code-named *Amerika*.

During this period Hitler began preparing the military machine against the one target that he had never lost sight of – the Soviet Union. By September 1940, he was discussing his decision to attack Russia in the spring the following year. By special order of the Führer, Chief engineer Fritz Todt, his army adjutant Lieutenant Colonel Engel and other headquarter staff officers and construction specialists were sent out to look for a suitable site for Hitler to direct his campaign against Russia. In November Todt had found a location and was instructed to build a huge fortress, bigger than anything else yet built.

It was emphasized however, because of its size and remarkable construction, it would take many months to complete. The site itself, known only by a handful of the Führer's closest staff, was situated deep inside the East Prussian forest of Gorlitz, a few miles east of a town called Rastenburg (now Ketrzyn in Poland). Before the area had been sealed off for a military barracks, it had been a place to relax for the people of the nearby town. The task of sending thousands of construction workers to build the new headquarters was left in the capable hands of the *Konstrukionsburo* with engineer Peter Behrens heading the construction team of *Organisation Todt* workers.

During the initial construction phase, the identity of the headquarters was camouflaged under the code name *Anlage Nord* (Camp North), and also *Chemische Werke Askania* (Askania Chemical Works). When building first began at *Anlage Nord*, two other headquarter sites were also chosen in Poland and underwent construction. They were known as *Anlage Mitte* (Installation Centre) near Tomaszow, and *Anlage Süd* (Installation South), near Krosno. The building of these two installations was not designed as a permanent headquarters for Hitler's forthcoming campaign, consequently they were never to match the huge concrete fortress of *Anlage Nord*. Instead they were purely as tunnels of reinforced concrete for Hitler's special headquarters train, *Führersonderzug Amerika*, with platforms and a few wooden huts scattered about.

A few hundred miles to the north, work continued on *Anage Nord*. For seven solid months, *Organisation Todt* labourers laid out a network of roads through the swampy malarial East Prussian landscape. They turned forest paths into a huge complex of wood and concrete bunkers and other buildings. Dormitory barracks for thousands of construction workers covered the area, with many teams working in shifts around the clock. Massive excavation machines dug out thousands of tons of earth, and huge amounts of steel and concrete filled the holes. At night the various buildings sites glowed with light, and occasionally detonations thundered through the forest.

In total, an area of 154,501 square metres was developed, with only four per cent of the area comprised bunkers. Hitler's headquarters covered 41,720 square metres. Of the 173,260 cubic metres of concrete laid, three-quarters of it was poured into Hitler's headquarters sites, whilst the remainder was laid in OKH and the Luftwaffe Command centres. On average, some 4,600 German OT workers and foreign labourers, which were all thoroughly vetted by the RSD, worked on the vast construction programme at any time. The peak period before Hitler's arrival was between September 1940 and June 1941.

Every day a stream of workers entered the construction site, labourers, builders, plumbers, electricians, telecommunication engineers, air conditioning specialists and architects. Miles of cables were laid and telecommunication installations were connected through a small telephone/telex exchange building. In total, three exchanges were set up and an independent telegraphy unit was installed at Heligenlinde, about fifteen miles to the west of Hitler's new headquarters.

Various barrack-type huts with mantels of brickwork and concrete were constructed, and plans were drawn up to reinforce their ceilings for protection against bomb splinters. Originally there were ten bunker constructed, each had been reinforced with two metres of concrete. The floor in the rear part of the bunker was sunk over two metres deep and was to be used for sleeping quarters. Inside the work bunkers a narrow corridor led to what was known as the workroom door. This door led to a small room which could house two desks, chairs and filing cabinets. The windows to these bunkers had steel shutters attached and could only be closed and bolted from the outside. The windowless dormitory bunkers had two entrances. Inside the cabins were panelled with light wood and the sleeping compartments were furnished with a bed, wash basin, fitted wardrobe and later connected by telephone. Near the entrance of the bunker, plumbers installed a small bathroom complete with waste pipe and running water.

Air ducting engineers installed ventilation machinery which drew fresh air through the ceiling. Air conditioning units were installed.

All the rooms also had electrical heating, and warm air could be circulated through the ventilation shafts. The ventilator proved to be noisy, but engineers found that if it was turned off the bunker became unbearably hot and stuffy. Those that were to occupy the bunkers were instructed to ensure that the ventilators remained on at all times, in spite of the terrible shrieking noise they made.

Elsewhere around the headquarters builders assembled the small guard houses, which were positioned at the three entrances to the installation, North, South and East. Barbed wire fencing surrounded the entire headquarters and blockhouses for guard personnel were built.

By the end of May, a full inspection was made of the new headquarters site, and on 6 June 1941 the 1st Battalion Flak Regiment 604 was moved to the Gorlizt Forest. The flak unit which was to protect Hitler's headquarters from possible aerial attack consisted of five batteries, three of which were equipped with 10.5cm guns and one each with 2cm and 3.7cm guns.

By the time the Russian invasion was unleashed on 22 June 1941, work on the headquarters still had not been completed. With word that the Führer might arrive any day, frantic measures were immediately undertaken to complete the finishing touches to the *Führerbunker*, and other important bunkers and buildings that were to house Hitler's staff during the conquest of Russia.

Chapter II

'And so to the East'

On 23 June 1941, just before midday Adolf Hitler and his headquarters entourage made their way through the sprawling streets of Berlin to Hitler's *Führersonderzug Amerika*. At half-past noon in the sweltering heat the twin locomotives consisting of fifteen or more coaches, guarded by two flak wagons, left for East Prussia hauling the Führer and his staff.

Throughout the night the various echelons of Supreme Headquarters followed *Amerika* either by rail or air. Just after midnight *Amerika* halted on a local line a few hundred yards from the headquarters perimeter fence. Boarding a column of waiting field vehicles Hitler was driven up to a forest and inside this forbidding, heavily guarded wood stood his new headquarters. During the train journey Hitler had decided to call it Wolf's Lair. When Hitler's secretary, Fraulein Christa Schroder inquired, 'Why Wolf again – just like the other headquarters?' Hitler replied, 'That was my code name in the years of struggle.'[1]

The Wolf's Lair installation was laid out on both sides of an asphalt road which passed west/east through the Gorlitz forest from Rastenburg and then on north-east to Angerburg. The forest was less than 2,000 metres across, and because there were so many meadows and open spaces scattered among the tall pine trees, it was essential to hang camouflage netting to hide the installation from aerial observation. Just north of the road was the railway line which passed through Rastenburg. For a number of years there had been a railway station in the small town of Gorlitz, south of the forest. For some time, tourists had visited the area using the rail network, but now this had been stopped. A rail siding was added to the original rail line at the station, and its building was added to throughout the summer of 1941. A longer ramp was built to accommodate the arrival and departure of *Amerika*.

It was 1.30 am when Hitler and staff entered the enclosure. Passing cordons of sentries of the FBB guarding the Görlitz forest, they moved through the outer perimeter barrier known as *Sperrkreis IV* (Security Zone IV), which was a high barbed wire fence enclosing an area of about 2.5 square kilometres and well hidden from the road. Installed menacingly along the fence were blockhouses, flak and machine-gun towers, and other defensive emplacements including a small minefield surrounding the compound. Again sentries patrolled the barrier here, as well as posts within the compound. Beyond the outer perimeter was an extensive number of concrete gun emplacements strategically emplaced at road junctions and covering access roads.

Security at the installation was multi-layered. There were essentially one outer and three inner security zones known as Security Zone I, Security Zone II, Security Zone III, and Security Zone IV, each complete with checkpoints and guards. A visitor entering Wolf's Lair passed through at least two, three or even four checkpoints on his way through to Hitler's Security Zone I, the inner sanctum of the headquarters. It was situated north of the Rastenburg/Angerburg tracks and road in the eastern part of Security Zone II. As one approached this well guarded enclosure, it too was surrounded by a fence and topped with barbed wire. Here, sentries manned the western and eastern entrance gates with a barrier, scrutinizing every person that wanted access.

Security Zone I consisted of huge concrete bunkers that loomed over an assortment of wooden huts. The bunkers were concealed from the air by painted designs on walls, foliage between buildings on poles and camouflage netting suspended from the tree tops. A Stuggart landscaping firm had been hired to install artificial trees, camouflage nets and artificial moss on top of buildings, over the concrete roads inside the installation, and wherever man-made structures might be visible from the air. The *Führersonderzug* too, was kept under cover of camouflage trees and nets when it stopped at Görlitz, the Wolf's Lair station. Chief of the OKW, General Wilhelm Keitel wrote in his memoirs:

> I have often flown over the site at various altitudes, but despite my precise knowledge of its location was never able to pin-point it from the air, except perhaps by the virtue of the lane leading through the forest and a single-track railway spur which had been closed to public traffic.[2]

Despite serious efforts to keep the headquarters secret, close observation of the area using aerial photography could locate the installation. But the

German security authorities could not know if the Russians would be able to determine that the buildings hidden among the trees were Hitler's Eastern Front headquarters. Nevertheless great efforts were made throughout the War to conceal it from enemy aerial reconnaissance.

Inside Security Zone I the Führer and his entourage from State, party and Wehrmacht came to live. On the military side, Keitel, General Alfred Jodl and aides, together with the newly appointed 'historian', Colonel Walter Scherff set up camp. Here the assorted huts served as a conference room, mess and administrative offices. There were guest quarters, a mail room, a communication bunker, a teahouse and there was even a cinema and plans for a sauna. Everyone lived and worked in wooden huts, barracks or concrete bunkers which were above ground and consisted of two or more rooms. Newly constructed roads and tracks criss-crossed the entire site, which were screened by many trees. Hitler's bunker (No.11), known as the *Führerbunker*, was the main structure in Security Zone I. His hut and bunker was hidden at the extreme northern end. In addition to the *Führerbunker*, many other bunkers had been erected. During the first construction phase, concrete and brick houses were built with windows and steel shutters.* Just south of the *Führerbunker* across a gravel path was a small building known as Kasino. I, a building which contained two dining rooms for the Führer and his inner circle. Between these two buildings was a flagstone walk, which was partly covered by camouflage netting suspended from the trees. The path ran south to an office/bunker for Keitel. South of Keitel's building was a long, barracks-type building for Jodl. West of the *Führerbunker* was a bunker/office/quarters for *Reichsleiter* Martin Bormann, head of Hitler's secretariat and Chief of Party Chancellery. Nearby, running parallel to the railway line and security fence stood *Reichsmarshall* Herman Göring's house.†

Throughout Security Zone I there were a wide range of buildings and plans for a host of other bunkers and barracks. On the main Security Zone I road, west of the Keitelbunker (No.7), were two bunker/barracks-type

---

* During the next construction period of the headquarters two tall bunkers were built to be used primarily as air raid shelters, barracks for the elements of the FBB manning and patrolling the outer perimeter with its machine-gun and anti-tank gun emplacements, and barracks for the *Führer-Flak-Abteilung* (Führer Anti-aircraft Detachment) manning the anti-aircraft batteries throughout the installation.

† During the War, Göring used his Wolf's Lair facility only occasionally, spending most of his time when he was in East Prussia on board his *Sonderzug Robinson*, about 65 kilometres away in the Romintern Forest.

buildings for the Führer's personnel and SS adjutants (No. 8) and another (No. 13) for his Wehrmacht adjutant. There were buildings for the Reich Press Chief, guests, men of the RSD (*Reichssicherheitsdienst*, Reich's Security Service) and *SS-Begleit-Kommando* (Escort command troops), and quarters for Hitler's inner circle including personal servants, and secretaries. Christa Schroder wrote:

> The blockhouses are scattered in the woods, grouped according to the work we do. Our sleeping bunker, as big as a railway compartment, is very comfortable-looking, panelled with a beautiful light-coloured wood … as the air conditioning noise bothered us … we have it switched off at night with the result that … we walk around with leaden limbs all next day. Despite all this it is wonderful except for an appalling plague of mosquitoes. The men are better protected by their long leather boots and thick uniforms; their only vulnerable point is the neck. Some of them go around all day with mosquito nets on. Wherever a mosquito turns up, it is hunted down. In the first few days this led to immediate problems of jurisdiction, as the Chief [Hitler] says it should be the Luftwaffe's job only. They say the small mosquitoes are replaced by a far more unpleasant sort at the end of June. God help us!
>
> It is almost too cool indoors … the forest keeps out the heat: you don't notice how much until you go out onto the street, where the heat clamps down on you.[3]

Security Zone II was a fenced encampment north and south of the Rastenburg-Angerburg road, inside the larger fenced area. Here too, the compound was entirely surrounded by high barbed wire fencing and was virtually camouflaged from the road. It housed the concrete and brick single storey houses of the *Wehrmachtfuhrungsstab* (Wehrmacht Leadership staff) or WFst, and the headquarters commandant, SS-Gruppenführer Hans Rattenhuber, and his staff. The majority of officers were housed in wooden huts around a simple country inn that was once used by the local inhabitants. There were two messes; heating plants, and a communication centre (telephone exchange). East of these buildings, still south of the road, there were concrete and brick houses for the Luftwaffe and Navy liaison officers and a two storey building for the drivers with garages at the ground level.

Walking through Security Zone II a visitor soon realised that the installation was far removed from the normal picture of a military headquarters. Everything had been undertaken by the designers to try and make the camp as comfortable as possible, including the living quarters. Inside the officers quarters for instance there were walls covered with ornate wooden panelling painted in cheerful colours. There were also built-in cupboards, glazed basins and baths with running water and even central heating.

There were several other installations in the general area of the Wolf's Lair, between 12 and 50 miles away. These installations served the needs of the Army High Command and its General Staff. The Luftwaffe High Command had its own headquarters onboard Göring's *Robinson*, *Reichsführer SS* Heinrich Himmler's *Sonderzug Heinrich* was shunted into a railway siding near Grossgarten (now Pozedre), and Foreign Minister Joachim von Ribbentrop's and State Security Dr Hans Heinrich Lammers' railway carriages were also parked there. In addition to a platform there were five small bunkers that served only as air-raid shelters, and were not habitable. In July 1941 Ribbentrop and Lammers managed to obtain a place away from the sweltering carriages. Ribbentrop took up headquarters in a mansion about five miles north-east of the Wolf's Lair, and seven miles south of the Army High Command headquarters *Mauerwald*.

The *Mauerwald* installation had been built in a dry, high pine forest and was regarded by those that worked and lived there as considerably healthier and more comfortable than the Führer's breezeless, fetid swampland. The site was divided into two sections, *Fritz* and *Quelle*, and separated by a road. General Staff officers were all encamped in *Fritz*, except for the supply section which was in *Quelle*, together with administrative offices. As at the Wolf's Lair, there were bunkers and hutments built into the forested area. Some 1,500 personnel worked just at *Mauerwald*.

The entire area surrounding the Wolf's Lair including the other headquarters installations were all integrated into the early warning system of *Air Fleet Reich*, land forces under the control of No. I Military District Command in Konigsberg. The Wolf's Lair however, was the most heavily defended site of them all by the *Führer-Luft-Nachrichten-Abteilung* (FLNA, Führer Signal Detachment), and a much strengthened FBB (later renamed the *Führer Begleit-Brigade*).

Deployed around the Wolf's Lair there were normally around 30 anti-aircraft guns, some 70 light MG34 machine-guns, between 16 and 21 tank guns, two heavy MG34 machine-guns, and four 7.5cm well dug-in tank guns. Tanks, mainly of the Pz.Kpfw.IIIs and Pz.Kpfw.IV types, were fully manned and armed, stationed both within and outside the outer perimeter.

Troop strength was estimated in the region of 1,570 officers and men. Security and guard duties along the fences of Restricted Security Zone I and II were the primary responsibility of the FBB units. They guarded partly inside and outside the Führer's headquarters. One entire platoon of the three guard companies was on active guard duty at any one time. Inside the fenced area, Security Zone I, the principal security forces were the RSD and the *SS-Begleit-Kommando*.

Rattenhuber and his deputy, *SS-Sturmbannführer* Peter Hogl, were in charge of Hitler's personal security. Permanent guards were posted all over Security Zone I. One SS sentry stood guarding the front of the *Führerbunker* day and night, whilst at the same time one RSD officer was in constant patrol. There was one RSD in front of the shorthand writers hut day and night, and one RSD patrol throughout Security Zone I from 10 am to 6 pm. The RSD officer patrolling the immediate area around the *Führerbunker* watched all entrances. He was ordered to prevent all disturbances around the bunker area, which included noise, and the entry of unauthorized persons. Hitler's personal adjutants, *SS-Obergruppenführer* Julius Schaub, *NSKK-Gruppenführer* Albert Bormann, Chief Wehrmacht Adjutant Lieutenant-General Rudolf Schmundt, *SS-Sturmbannführer* Otto Gunsche and *SS-Sturmbannführer* Richard Schulze-Kossens used the RSD guard for small errands and runner services. The RSD officers had to make sure that unauthorized persons, including persons on duty or quartered in Security Zone I, did not walk about the compound unnecessarily, in particular in the vicinity of the *Führerbunker*.

One of Keitel's aides remembers vividly that he had to have permission on every occasion to go to the *Führerbunker*. Identification papers were always scrutinized and persons or visitors were always escorted to wherever they needed to be taken. An individual found without a valid pass was immediately escorted off the premises and questioned. Only persons working in Security Zone I or serving the Führer directly were allowed by the RSD officers to enter the compound regularly. It was strictly forbidden to allow anyone to enter the Zone without a pass, not even if they were chaperoned with someone else with a pass, except if they were escorted through the gate by an RSD officer. Everyone who required access needed to obtain new or additional passes either by express permission of the Chief Wehrmacht adjutant Schmundt, his deputy, *SS-Obergruppenführer* Schaub or his deputy, or personally from the headquarters commandant. Security measures were so stringent inside the Führer's compound that motor traffic was restricted to cars of persons holding high ranking positions and Reich ministers and leaders. These and their drivers, including all passengers, no matter what rank they held, all had to have valid passes. Those without a pass were ordered out of the vehicle and instructed to wait outside the gate.

Despite the tight security, it was possible in those early days of the War to accidentally wander through into Security Zone I. Such an incident occurred when a Colonel got off the local train near the compound, thinking he was in the army's *Mauerwald* installation, and casually walked into the inner sanctum. Once inside, he found the officer's mess and ordered some breakfast. Sitting at the table he was surprised to see Hitler's Navy Aide, Rear-Admiral Karl Jesco von Puttkamer. When Puttkamer wanted to know why he was sitting in the officer's mess in Security Zone I of the Wolf's Lair, the Colonel refused at first to believe that he was not at *Mauerwald*, until Puttkamer pointed Hitler out to him, strolling outside.

Although such cases were very rare, there were occasions when labourers working on the site accidentally wandered into forbidden areas. One Polish labourer left his place of work without permission and took a short cut on his way home. As he passed through some trees he was spotted by a sentry guarding the outer perimeter of Security Zone IV, and was shot dead on the spot.

Though the Wolf's Lair was unusually close to the front, those living there could never quite come to terms with the loneliness of the place. The whole area was so vast that even with the atmosphere charged with high military drama, everyone still appeared to feel isolated and perplexed. Relatively comfortable as it was, those living inside the compound could not quite rid themselves of the feeling of being behind the wire, as in prison. Even the amenities such as a Turkish bath, an officer's club, cafes, a cinema and swimming bath could not dissipate their feeling of entrapment.

Some, however, tried their best to escape from what they saw as the prison of concrete and wood. Once they had got through the maze of barbed wire, minefields, and the string of security cordons, they found good walks in the local neighbourhood. Frequently officers and personnel alike would be seen strolling through the surrounding woods and around the lakes of the East Prussian countryside, and sometimes basking lazily in the sun during the early hours of the afternoon. The deputy chief of operations for the OKW, General Walther Warlimont, for instance, regularly took to strolling through the forests and around the lakes. The countryside, he later recalled, with its well managed forests, heath lands, tree-shaded roads, rivers and lakes always gave him repose.

Inside the Wolf's Lair however, life continued routinely and there was hardly any respite. Almost as soon as the various staff sections of the army moved into Security Zone II they set to work collecting and collating information for the vital continuation of the War. As usual practice in the running of military operations from the supreme headquarters, a considerable part of the work was left in the capable hands of General Warlimont of Section L. His department was given the task of collecting reports each morning and evening from the Wehrmacht, Luftwaffe and Navy and sorting and dispatching them by courier to the Chief of Operations, General Jodl, together with their attached situation maps that were brought up to date by the staff's draughtsman. These reports, together with the attached situation maps were shown at the midday war conference over in Security Zone I, which was held each day in the Führer's presence. Here, they also discussed the morning reports from the various High Commands.

All the conferences that took place in Security Zone I were held in the *Keitelbunker* (until the autumn of 1942). During these military meetings it was customary for Jodl to outline the war situation, including the army's position when the army's Commander-in-Chief, Field-Marshal von Brauchitsch and Chief of the General Staff of the Army Colonel General Franz Halder were themselves participating. All War conferences lasted an average of three hours and the evening conferences never less than one hour. Any orders or particular instructions the Führer issued on these occasions were dispatched after the conference that same evening by the OKW Operations Staff to the quarters concerned. Liaison officers were responsible for ensuring that their sections in Berlin had received any information and were working and adhering to those orders accordingly. All communications including the daily Wehrmacht reports, and also that of the press, party and state authorities would be dispatched to Berlin and sent to the various offices. Vital military communiqués were generally sent directly from the Wolf's Lair to the particular military field headquarters of the army group by telegram and dealt with immediately by the General Staff, who in turn would dispatch them to the supreme commander.

At the Wolf's Lair everyone watched nervously as reports of *Barbarossa*, the codename for the invasion of the Soviet Union, victoriously forged ahead. Within hours of the initial invasion of Russia, the German spearheads, with their brilliant co-ordination of all arms, had pulverized bewildered Russian border formations. Both OKW and OKH looked upon these first exhilarating days of the campaign as confirming the aura of invincibility that had not been enjoyed by any other army since Napoleon unleashed his forces against Russia.

By July 1941, the German Northern, Central and Southern Groups had bulldozed their way across vast areas of Russia and were achieving momentous victories on all fronts. In Army Group Centre, both Wehrmacht and Waffen-SS troops, spearheaded by the 2nd and 3rd Panzer Group, penetrated through Belorussia almost as far as Smolensk, a sprawling city on the Warsaw–Moscow highway. When they reached the city, they stood a mere 400 miles from the greatest prize of them all – Moscow. Enjoying the staggering successes, Hitler was seen taking leisurely strolls the compound of Security Zone I, and even taking time to chat familiarly with the labourers that were still working on the never ending building programme. At mealtimes, which were always a big occasion, the Führer seemed relaxed, but was noticeably uncertain on his objectives in Russia.

The list of guests, of whom only a few at a time could dine with Hitler in Dining room No.1, which was housed in the building Kasino I (No.10), just south of the Führerbunker, included Keitel, his adjutant Major John Freyend, Jodl and his adjutant Major Waizenegger, Schaub, Schmundt, the brothers Bormann, Otto Dietrich, Minister Walther Hewel, General Karl Bodenschatz, Dr Hans Karl von Hasselbach, Major-General Walther Scherff, Hitler's personal physician Dr Theo Morell, the Reich Photo Reporter, Staff Leaders *SS-Gruppenführer* Rattenhuber, Helmut Sudermann, Chief Pilot *SS-Gruppenführer* Hans Baur and pilot Gaim, Major Weiss, Personal adjutant *SS-Sturmbannführer* Fritz Darges, *SS-Sturmbannführer* Peter Hogl, Captain Gerhard von Szymonski, Captain Fuchs, Hitler's trusted chauffeur *SS-Sturmbannführer* Erich Kempka, *SS-Hauptsturmführer* Georg Friedrich Hans Pfeiffer, District Leader Heinz Lorenz, Judge Muller, Lorenz, and the headquarters photographer Lieutenant Walter Frentz. In all there were a total of 38 guests, all of which vied for favour with the Führer. In dining room No.2, dined ten shorthand writers and their typists, 23 aides, valets and typists. Hitler's secretary, Christa Schroder wrote:

> Shortly after 10 am we two [Gerda Daranowski Andi] go to the mess bunker – along [a] whitewashed room sunk half-underground, so that glaze covered windows are very high up. A table for twenty people takes up the entire length of the room; here the chief takes his lunch and supper with his Generals, his General Staff officers, adjutants, and doctors. At breakfast and afternoon coffee we two girls are also there. The chief sits facing the maps of Russia hanging on the opposite wall.
>
> We wait in this No.1 dining room each morning until the chief arrives for breakfast from the map room, where meantime he has been briefed on the war situation. Breakfast for him, I might add, is just a glass of milk and mashed apple: somewhat modest and unpretentious.
>
> Afterward we go at 1.pm to the General situation conference in the map room ... the statistics on enemy aircraft and tanks destroyed are announced – the Russians seem to have enormous numbers, as we have already annihilated

over 3,500 aircraft and over 1,000 tanks including some heavy ones, forty tonners. They have been told to fight to the end and shoot themselves if need be ... If there is nothing important to be done, we sleep a few hours after lunch so we are bright and breezy for the rest of the day, which usually drags on till the cows come home. Then, around 5 pm, we are summoned to the chief and plied with cakes by him. The one who grabs the most cakes gets his commendation! This coffee break most often goes on to 7 pm, frequently even longer. Finally we lie low in the vicinity until the chief summons us to his study where there is a small get together with coffee and cakes again in his more intimate circle ... I often feel so feckless and superfluous here. If I consider what I actually do all day, the shattering answer is: absolutely nothing. We sleep, eat, drink, and let people talk to us, if we are too lazy to talk ourselves...

This morning the chief said that if ever the German soldier deserved a laurel wreath it was for this campaign. Everything is going far better than we hoped. There have been many strokes of good fortune, for example, that the Russians met us on the frontier and did not first lure us far into their hinterland with all the enormous transport and supply problems that would certainly have involved.[4]

Such were the successes at the front, nearly everyone at the Wolf's Lair thought that victory would soon come and that they would be home by winter. Even during these sweltering days of July, Hitler openly declared that the Red Army was doomed. Life at the headquarters continued more or less unchanged. As usual, his intimate staff eagerly visited every day for breakfast, lunch, and in the evening relaxed in either the *Führerbunker* or over in the teahouse, a short walk south of the *Führerbunker*. Generally, the tea house was the scene of his famous table talks. One of Hitler's secretaries noted in her diary:

I really must start writing down what the chief says. It's just that these sessions go on for ages and afterward you are just too limp and lifeless to write anything. The night before last, when we left the chief's bunker, it was already light. We did not turn in even then, as ordinary people would have, but made for the kitchen, ate a few cakes, and then strolled for two hours toward the rising sun, past farmyards and paddocks, past hillocks glowing with red and white clover in the morning sun, a fairyland on which you just could not feast your eyes enough; and then back to bed. We are incapable of getting up before 2 or 3 pm. A crazy life ... A strange calling like ours probably never [will] be seen again; we eat, we drink, we sleep, now and then we type a bit, and meantime keep him company for hours on end. Recently we did make ourselves a bit useful – we picked some flowers, so that his bunker does not look too bare.[5]

The OKW war diarist Helmuth Greiner wrote a private letter of the conditions inside the headquarters during that summer of 1941:

We're being plagued by the most awful mosquitoes. It would be hard to pick a more senseless site than this – deciduous forest with marshy pools, sandy ground, and stagnant lakes, ideal for those loathsome creatures. On top of which, our bunkers are cold and damp. We freeze to death at night, can't get to sleep because of the humming of the air conditioning and the terrible draught it makes, and we wake up every morning with a headache. Our underwear and uniforms are always cold and clammy.[6]

Confidently though, Greiner hoped, like so many others, to leave the barbed-wire entanglements of the Wolf's Lair forever. In his diary in July 1941 he predicted that the Red Army would be annihilated and that Germany would triumph before Christmas. But in spite of the confidence throughout the headquarters there was emerging evidence of growing Russian resistance. Even at the daily war conference Hitler himself could not conceal his worries about the increasing extent of the enemy's armament. Prior to the invasion, his experts in the field had told him nothing of Russia's enormous array of armour. In his bunker he was seen by his adjutants to be concerned at the prospect of a major calamity on the Eastern Front, and was brooding. On 21 July Greiner wrote in his OKW diary:

Nobody discussed this [the Russian campaign] at lunch with the Führer yesterday. At first he was very taciturn, and just brooded … then he came to life and delivered a monologue of an hour or more on our brave and gallant Italian Allies and the worries they are causing him … you can't help being astonished at his brilliant judgement and clear insights. He looks in the best health and seems well, although he seldom gets to bed before 5 or 6 am.[7]

During the first week of August, Hitler complained of not feeling well. On 7 August one of Hitler's secretaries noticed how unwell he looked. After breakfast she watched as the Führer struggled to walk over from Kasino I to the *Führerbunker*. That same morning Hitler visited the map room and suddenly felt faint and then began vomiting. For days he had been steadily getting worse and now had diarrhoea, severe stomach pains, nausea, and a high fever. His personal physician Dr Morell told him he had contracted bacillary dysentery from the surrounding swamplands. Morell noted in his diary that life in the bunker had caused his rapid decline in health. On the following day he was confined to his bed and due to his complaint was allowed no more than one soft boiled egg, mashed potato, and strawberries for supper.

Despite not feeling well, Hitler was determined not to be confined to his dreary sleeping quarters. After he had received his morning injection he would drag himself from his bunker over to the *Keitelbunker* and attended the war conference, which was now being held each morning and evening. At these long drawn out conferences he sat at a long narrow oak map table with the staff crowded round him, watching intently as he scoured the maps of western Russia, trying to plot the next military breakthrough of the Wehrmacht. Although Hitler appeared pale and drawn he tried to conceal his ailments and dominated the conferences. The first weeks of August were difficult for the military and despite frantic appeals from his Generals to abandon the *Barbarossa* directive and divert the main thrust of the campaign on Moscow, Hitler held his nerve and warned them of the serious consequences of such an action.

However firm Hitler was at the military conferences his declining health was becoming more apparent. He even began complaining that he found them hard-going and he became increasingly incapable of arguing with his Generals. At one particular conference held in early August he had to call for the assistance of Morell. His ears were buzzing and he complained of terrible headaches. His little doctor resorted to using the medieval method of applying leeches into his ear in order to try and lower his blood pressure. After his ears had bled for a considerable time bandages were applied to his head. Hitler vainly refused to be seen wearing the bandages around the headquarters, and as a consequence decided to eat alone in his bunker.

Over the next few days Hitler appeared to be feeling much better. Although he stated he felt like he had recovered from his bout of dysentery, his staff, still thought he looked pale and drawn. On 19 August Morell recorded in his diary:

The bunker is damp and unhealthy, the temperature just right for growing fungi; once, my boots were mouldy after being left two days, and my clothes got clammy in the bedroom. New bunker walls always sweat quantities of water at first ... then there are the colds caused by the draught of the extractor fans. I pointed out all that after just four days in the bunker ... people got chest constrictions, anaemia, and general bunker psychosis. I reminded him that I had initially recommended more frequent motor journeys or five days in his special train, a change of scenery to somewhere at a greater altitude. At that time the Führer declared that this wasn't on because of the centralization of his signals equipment, etc, I also suggested he spend fourteen days at the Berghof.[8]

18 August was a beautiful summer's day, and for the first time in five weeks Hitler's staff watched as he ventured outside his bunker and strolled with Josef Goebbels along his favourite stretch of the compound. The installation was a hive of activity and a number of areas were still a building site. *Organization Todt* workers were labouring continuously on new buildings, and those still working inside Security Zone I often able to get a glimpse of the Führer for the first time since his arrival in June. Although security was as stringent as ever inside Hitler's compound the labourers were able to walk about, as long as they did not walk in close proximity to the bunkers, especially as the *Führer* and *Keitelbunkers*. Guards were positioned at the entrances of both these buildings at all times and security was tightened during the military conferences. No one was allowed to pass too close to the windows of the buildings either. If the workers had to quickly enter a building because of an emergency, such as a broken water pipe for instance, security officers had to accompany them. During the summer of 1941, additional fences were erected in order to cordon off the construction sites within the compounds of Security Zone I and II. RSD guards were present guarding the entrances to the construction sites and a pass was required by every workman. Though Hitler trusted his German workforce, he was under no illusion as to the risks posed by anyone that entered the Wolf's Lair as a visitor. When he was seen wondering around the installation, he was always protected by his trusted bodyguards, both near him and at some distance away patrolling the local wooded terrain, scrutinizing the area.

Security was further intensified at the headquarters when dignitaries and other high-ranking personalities arrived, such as on 25 August for the visit of Benito Mussolini. An excited Hitler greeted the *Duce* at the headquarters station, and the entourage, consisting of open top Mercedes painted in dull olive-grey, drove the short distance back into Security Zone I. Hitler did not waste any time and showed his Italian guest around his new headquarters. Later over a cold buffet in the garden, just outside the tea house, Hitler spoke incessantly for hours of the crusade against Bolshevism. He also openly admitted the failures of military intelligence and the immense size of the Red Army, but predicted that victory would certainly be secured by the spring of 1942. Hitler's staff were also becoming impatient to leave the dreary surroundings of the Gorlitz Forest. At the end of August, Christa Schroder wrote:

> Our stay at the headquarters gets longer and longer. First we thought we would be back in Berlin by the end of July, then they talked of mid-October; and now they are already saying we will not get away before the end of October, if even then. It is already quite cool here, like Autumn, and if it occurs to the Chief to spend the winter here we shall all be frozen. This protracted bunker existence can't be doing us any good. The Chief does not look too well either, he gets little fresh air and now he is oversensitive to the sun and wind the moment he goes out in his car for a few hours. I would have loved to stay in Galicia – we were all in favour of it – but security there is not good enough...
>
> The whole countryside there is freer. Here in the forest it all crowds in on you after a while. Besides, there you didn't have the feeling that you were locked in; you saw the peasants working in the fields and it made you feel free, while here we keep stumbling on sentries and are forever showing our identity cards. Well, I suppose that wherever we are we're always cut off from the world – in Berlin, at the Berghof, or on our travels. It is always the same sharply defined circle, always the circuit inside the fence.[9]

On 28 August at 8 pm, both Hitler and Mussolini drove out of Security Zone I to the headquarters airfield where they flew to General von Rundstedt's command post at Uman. Much of the Führer's headquarters staff including his intimate circle stayed behind. His secretaries complained bitterly of the monotony and without Hitler's presence they found that many of the Generals frowned upon the women staff.

By early September, Hitler arrived back from the Ukraine infused with confidence. He began his first war conference of the month displaying determination and optimism. As predicted reports from the front confirmed that the *Wehrmacht* was indeed achieving a number of great successes, and there was even talk of the necessity of reaching Moscow before the onset of winter.

Hitler's confidence was further bolstered by news that Kiev had fallen on 19 September. With Kiev captured, the Wehrmacht were now in a good position to seize the strategically important oil-producing Caucasus Mountains and the Donetz Basin with its industrialized areas. But Hitler had already been drawing up plans for the resumption of operations against

Moscow. He told his Generals buoyantly that the Soviets would be taken by surprise at such an audacious plan so late in the year. Field-Marshal Fedor von Bock, commander of Army Group Centre, and a frequent visitor that summer at the headquarters, had for weeks been continually badgering Hitler incessantly on the need to attack Moscow. Now, as autumn was fast approaching, he began to change his mind. In front of Bock with maps of central Russia sprawled out across the narrow oak table, Hitler adamantly told the dumbfounded General that the last act of *Barbarossa* would be fought out at Moscow.

The organization for the final assault on the capital was an extraordinary feat in itself: General Guderian's Panzer Group had to return to the Ukraine and General Hoeppner's taks had to taken out of the Leningrad Front. Within just two weeks, Army Group Centre was ready.

During the early hours of 30 September, the Wolf's Lair received word that the first phase of 'Operation Typhoon', the attack on Moscow, had begun. General Guderian's Panzer Group was launched north-eastwards towards Orel, from where it would thrust north behind Yeremoneko's Bryansk Front. Two days later, on 2 October, the rest of the Army Group rolled forward.

Hitler was seen nervously pacing the *Führerbunker* that day. He spoke little, except to ask for weather reports. He knew perfectly well that the sub-zero temperatures and snow would soon have a role to play in the East. Nevertheless, the news at the war conference was good: Field Marshal Fedor von Bock's forces were surrounding Red Army formations and destroying them. Emboldened by this hopeful news from the front, Hitler and staff left the headquarters on 3 October for the long haul back to Berlin. Within twenty-four hours *Amerika* was bearing them back to their East Prussia headquarters. As soon as Hitler arrived in his bunker he immediately wanted a progress report on 'Typhoon'. It seemed that his forces were continuing to reap the awards and were enjoying significant successes. In front of his staff that evening, his face, which was previously wan and withdrawn, was now beaming with confidence. His staff noticed that he was able to relax more and was able to converse with them all. Over dinner on 6 October he was again in a cheerful mood, and he even made light-hearted jokes, something that he had not done for some time.

The next day however, tension once more gripped the headquarters at the midday conference as Bock's forces were in the process of completing a huge encirclement around Vyazma. Although *Reichsführer* Heinrich Himmler was guest of honour that day, celebrating his birthday with the Führer, Hitler was very nervous and was unable to eat. To add to his increasing trepidation and concerns over the military events transpiring in the East, Hitler was standing beneath the camouflage overhang between Kasino I and the *Führerbunker* when the first snow shower fell.

In spite the arrival of bad weather, Hitler was still displaying an iron nerve in front of his generals. On 9 October his secretaries found him in a friendly mood, and he even took a stroll around the perimeter fence of the compound. Over lunch that day Jodl remarked that the Führer did not seem disturbed by the events that were transpiring in front of Moscow. He himself had no doubt that the Soviets were finished.

Hitler appeared convinced his force would triumph over the Red Army. When Hitler's Reich Minister for Munitions Dr Fritz Todt and Gauleiter Fritz Saukel dined with the Führer on 17 October, they were also confident that victory would be attained. Nonetheless their unfailing optimism could not hide the fact that bad weather was stalling the *Wehrmacht*. During the conferences Hitler and his staff had to listen to a catalogue of reports confirming that Bock's Army Group Centre had been badly hit by an unusually early winter. The Russian countryside had been turned into a quagmire with the roads and fields becoming virtually impassable. It was confirmed that all the roads leading to Moscow had become boggy swamps. Although tanks and other tracked vehicles managed to push through the mire at a slow pace, trucks and wheeled vehicles were hopelessly stuck up to their axles in deep, boggy mud. Despite frantic efforts by thousands of soldiers to pull them free, the progress was painfully slow. To make matters worse, as the rain turned to snow troops begun to shiver for the first time. The advance had gone from a glorious display of military might to a slow, pitiful slog eastward. A winter on the Eastern Front now seemed inevitable.

As the situation worsened, at mealtimes Hitler once more brooded. On 30 October on the way to the map room he met Admiral Wilhelm Canaris and asked him with concern if he had any news on the condition of the front. Canaris explained in no uncertain terms that the situation was indeed bad and that the troops were struggling. The next day on 1 November, snow settled for the first time at the headquarters. All over the installation, the freezing temperatures prompted thoughts of their brave legions fighting in the East. Over the next few days, as Bock's forces pushed forward through a blizzard, Hitler could not relax until word had reached him of their success. The first report had confirmed that the advance had gone well, but once more it faltered. Day by day, the elements of disaster fused – the German offensive was burning itself out.

On 24 November Bock telephoned Hitler requesting permission for another assault despite the appalling weather. As Hitler waited for word of Bock's success another even greater crisis began to befall the *Wehrmacht*. To the outrage of Hitler, Field Marshal von Rundstedt was forced to evacuate the smouldering city of Rostov, the gateway to the Caucasus. Red with anger the Führer sent one of his adjutants immediately over to Bunker 16 to the teleprinter exchange to telegraph an urgent message to Rundstedt instructing him not to move one foot back. Later that evening, the disgruntled Field Marshal cabled back insisting that he could not hold on, and if the Führer did not withdraw his order he should find someone to replace him. The message was greeted with anger and recrimination and sealed the fate of Rundstedt. Without even consulting Field Marshal von Brauchitsch Hitler hastily cabled back and told Rundstedt that he was agreeing to his request and that he should give up his command immediately.

Over the next few days Hitler hardly ventured from his bunker. Other than attending the war conferences, he spent most of his time shut away. Inside his bunker he became increasingly perturbed by the situation on the Eastern Front. Yet the gloom caused by the fall of Rostov soon paled into insignificance by depressing news of the drive on Moscow. In freezing conditions the entire central front began to disintegrate in the snow. In many areas there was startling evidence that soldiers were reluctant to emerge from their shelters during the blizzards to fight. Hundreds of tanks were abandoned in the drifting snow, and the crews had retreated in panic. In the map room red arrows were covering every map. An OKW staff officer recalled seeing the situation maps and how the Red Army arrows dominated the overall picture. Dejection and dismay swept the German supreme command. Von Brauchitsch was so discouraged by the unfolding nightmare in front of the Red capital that many believed he would resign. Even Hitler himself was having trouble dealing with the setback. General Halder noted in his war diary: 'He refuses outright to take any account of the figures and strengths, and insists that our superiority is proved by the number of prisoners taken.'[10] Jodl himself quietly admitted that victory could not be achieved before Christmas.

On the evening of 8 December Hitler reluctantly left East Prussia with his headquarters staff for important business in the Reich capital. A week later *Amerika* was steaming back towards the headquarters. During the journey Hitler openly admitted that he was deeply concerned that the bulk of his force had no proper winter provisions for winter warfare, but despite this, he was determined to halt any more withdrawals. When he arrived back at the Wolf's Lair he immediately set about dictating a halt order to Halder so that the General could pass the information over by telephone. Troops of Army Group Centre were told that they were not to give one yard to the enemy.

Hitler's 'Halt Order' immediately caused consternation at the headquarters. As a direct consequence protests began emanating from commanders that saw a withdrawal as their only chance of salvation. Von Brauchitsch for one was totally opposed to Hitler's order. On 19 December, during a two-hour argument Hitler could no longer tolerate Brauchitsch and decided to relieve the weary Field Marshal of his command. Two hours later, to the astonishment of his war staff Hitler announced that he had decided to take over command of the army himself. For the first time in many days he appeared pleased with his decision and now could personally direct his troops. In his eyes the generals were the only threat to victory in the East. During nearly every war conference their incessant requests for a strategic retreat aggravated him. He had not dared to leave his headquarters, fearing that without his competent leadership the Eastern Front would degenerate into a panic flight.

Christmas festivities at the Wolf's Lair were sombre. On Christmas Eve, the Panzer ace General Heinz Guderian reported that he had only 40 tanks in his entire command. General Hoepner's Group had only one strength of more than 15 tanks, but still Hitler forbade them to withdraw. Hewel wrote: 'A dispirited Christmas. Führer's thoughts are elsewhere. No candles lit.'[11] On Christmas day, Hitler received his staff in turn, and handed them an envelope with a small amount of *Reichsmarks* inside. Despite greeting them with a firm handshake and a smile his staff noticed that he looked uncharacteristically detached.

On New Year's eve, General Field Marshal Gunther von Kluge began telephoning the headquarters, requesting permission for minor withdrawals. Hitler refused outright. That evening supper was served late. Afterwards Hitler fell fast asleep, exhausted by the day's events. As the last minutes of 1941 ticked away, his staff gathered quietly in the mess and waited for him to emerge. But since 11.30 pm Hitler had been on the telephone listening once again to Kluge appealing for the freedom to withdraw his troops. For three hours Hitler argued with his Field Marshal, explaining in no uncertain terms the need to stand fast. It was not until 2.30 am that Hitler appeared over at the tea house to greet his intimate staff. Weary-eyed, he slumped exhausted into a soft chair. In the background the phonograph was playing Bruckner's Seventh. Christa Schroder wrote:

On New Year's eve we were all in a cheerful enough mood at supper in the No.2 mess. After that we were ordered over to the regular tea session, where we found a very weary chief, who nodded off after a while. So we accordingly kept very quiet, which completely stifled what high spirits we had. We entered the New Year greetings with doom-laden faces … I just can't describe it, at any rate it was so ghastly that I broke down in tears in my bunker, and when I went back over to the mess I ran into a couple of lads of the escort command, who of course saw at once I had been crying – which set me off all over again, where upon they tried to comfort me with words and alcohol, successfully. And then we all sang a sea shanty at the top of our voices – 'At anchor off Madagascar, and we've got the plague abroad.'[12]

Chapter III

'Triumph or Die'

Following the traumatic events before Moscow, the New Year brought fresh hope and optimism. Those closest to the Führer saw that his iron leadership had, in effect stabilized the front. Even some of Hitler's bitterest critics, who had argued persistently about withdrawals, were amazed at his grand strategy. Hitler's policy to hold his battered and frost-bitten forces in front of the Red capital had saved ground, but at an alarming cost in men and materiel. The Red Army, as he had predicted, finally ran out of steam because of the harsh weather, and were unable to achieve any deep penetration into the German lines. Consequently, this had saved Bock's Army Group Centre from complete destruction. Although Hitler was to later say that the battle of Moscow was the finest hour, his army had in fact failed to capture the city, crucified by the Russian winter and by fanatical enemy resistance. Bock's failure to capture Moscow was essentially owing to the remarkable Russian recovery and their winter offensive. The battle had completely transformed the *Wehrmacht* from its glorious days in June 1941. Even Hitler himself could not mask the doubts about completing the huge task of beating the Red Army, despite his outward display of optimism at the war conferences. At mealtimes he appeared tense and uneasy beneath the avalanche of work that had descended upon him since taking command of the Army. Those working with him could see the gradual alteration in his temper and appearance. Hewel told a friend:

He is not the man he was. He has grown gloomy and obdurate. He will shrink from no sacrifice and show no mercy or forgiveness. You would not recognize him if you saw him.[13]

For the ensuing weeks Hitler's thoughts at the war conferences totally revolved around planning for the spring offensive. The Wolf's Lair was a hive of activity, especially the daily war conferences. During these long, drawn out sessions there was a widespread feeling of pessimism on the Eastern Front. But doubts were hardly ever raised.

On 7 February, Reich Minister for Munitions Fritz Todt entered the snow-covered compound of Security Zone I and reported to the Führer. After a short conference they had supper, and then continued their lengthy discussion with a large group, talking about Germany's war economy. The next morning, strained and fatigued from spending a very long night in the company of the Führer, Todt was driven out to the Rastenburg airfield to catch his Heinkel back to Berlin. Later that morning, Hitler was handed a message to say that Todt's Heinkel had crashed on take-off killing him instantly. News of the tragedy sent shock waves through the entire headquarters. Hitler appeared desolate at the loss. Over the breakfast table he nevertheless appeared unmoved by the minister's untimely death, and spoke about who would be the most suitable candidate to replace him. Although everyone agreed he was irreplaceable, there was one man the Führer had confidence in as his successor, Albert Speer, his trusted architect and beloved friend. On 9 February Speer was appointed successor to minister Todt.

The following day Hitler left the headquarters and returned to Berlin to attend Todt's funeral. When he returned to East Prussia on 15 February he was depressed and bad tempered. The snow and the arctic temperatures had deepened his despondency. Hitler's secretary described the mood inside the compound as bleak:

> After two days of warmer weather the temperature suddenly dropped again … the chief is always dog-tired, but he won't go to bed, and this is often a torment for the rest of us. We used to play records most evenings, and then you could fall back on your own thoughts; but since Todt's unfortunate end times for playing music have been few and far between.[14]

His secretaries were finding life at the headquarters increasingly difficult and this included the conversation, which they often considered tedious. They noticed that the Führer had changed since the traumatic events in the East. The winter crisis had undoubtedly seriously undermined his health, but in front of everyone he still showed that he would not be deterred from the mammoth task ahead. For him there could be no rest until victory was achieved. Despite his resolution, visitors to the Wolf's Lair found him tired and drawn. Over dinner he spoke persistently of the appalling winter as an ordeal successfully mastered, and he continued to pour scorn on his pessimistic commanders and blamed Brauchitsch for most of the setbacks. In his eyes, a number of his cowardly generals had completely sabotaged the entire plan of Barbarossa. Hitler said that Brauchitsch wanted prestige victories instead of real ones. He announced with fervour and excitment that the thaw in the East had begun and this would pave the way to final victory.

With the coming German spring offensive Hitler's health improved, he slowly regained his confidence and those that saw him daily felt that the worst on the Eastern Front was now over. Throughout March, the gradual German recovery in Russia continued until the spring mud and floods brought both sides to a temporary standstill. This enabled Hitler and staff time to draw up meticulous plans for the new offensive. In a three-hour conference, Hitler said that the summer offensive codenamed 'Blue', would commence with a southward thrust along the Don River towards Stalingrad. Following the capture of Stalingrad he planned using the city as an anchor, and to send the mass of his Panzer force south to occupy the Caucasus, where it would be used to cut off vital Russian oil supplies. The directive, dictated by Hitler himself was to be executed in two stages. The first part of the summer operation was a determined all-out drive of successive enveloping thrusts along the Kursk–Voronezh axis, where it was to destroy the Soviet southern flank and carry on to the Don River. The second part was the advance to Stalingrad and across the lower Don into the Caucasus. For this operation Army Group South would be divided. He ordered General List's Army Group A south, toward Rostov and the Caucasus, while General Weichs' Army Group B would be responsible for the drive across the lower Don to the Volga and into Stalingrad. It would be in the Caucasus, Hitler said, that they would ensure the Reich's survival in the War and bring about the ultimate victory he was yearning for.

On 20 April, Hitler's birthday, he diverted some of his attention from the coming summer offensive and received a number of guests at the headquarters. Göring, Ribbentrop, Milch, Raeder, and a group of other officials and guests attended his birthday held in a dining room which was set out with tablecloths and flowers. The headquarters officers and staff celebrated the occasion with cups of real coffee and a glass of Piesporter Goldtropfchen. After lunch Hitler and his guests were led out of Security Zone I where just on the edge of the forest they marvelled at a demonstration of the first two Tiger tanks.

Four days later Hitler gathered his headquarters staff for the long journey to Bavaria. His visit was not to rest in the solitude of his Berghof mountain retreat, as prescribed by Morell, but to prepare a major speech before the

Reichstag. By the time he arrived back at the Wolf's Lair the German spring offensive had finally been unleashed in the Crimea, on 8 May. During the following days Hitler and his generals watched as the high drama unfolded in the map room. At first, reports brought encouraging signs. But as the Russians intensified their resistance, telephone calls from anxious commanders began to flood the communications room appealing (in vain) to withdraw. To the outrage of Hitler, Von Bock once again – as he had done before Moscow the previous year – requested an urgent withdrawal from Kharkov. An angry Hitler told his staff that Bock was a defeatist. The offensive, he argued, was to continue as planned and his generals would just have to keep their nerve if they were to succeed. For the next few days the headquarters was in crisis. Hitler would emerge each day from the conference room pale and tired after arguing with his staff for hours. He was convinced that his forces should hold Kharkov at all costs and told them it would be destroyed. By the 22nd, that obstinate belief became reality. He was handed a report that thousands of his troops with a massive assemblage of armour had encircled Red Army formations and taken some 240,000 prisoners. That day, Hitler exultantly left his *Führerbunker* as the victor of Kharkov. Over at the *Keitelbunker* he openly marvelled at his military genius and the victory he had just won for his generals. Those that saw him that day found him beaming with confidence.

Emboldened by the first military victory of 1942, Hitler appeared convinced more than ever at the war conferences that the coming Blue offensive would be equally successful. The Caucasus, he predicted, was where the Russian bear would suffer its bloodiest defeat. For many months his generals had argued with him and opposed his grand strategy, but now he would prove them wrong.

On 28 June, Operation Blue began in earnest. At the midday war conference there was a widespread feeling of anxious activity as news bulletins began to come through from the front lines. The 2nd and 4th Panzer Army opened up the Blue offensive. Almost immediately the Panzers smashed their way through lines of Red Army defences and drove at breakneck speed east of Kursk and pushed toward Voronezh, reaching the outskirts of the smouldering city in four days. Following the capture of the city 4th Panzer then swung south-east along the Don where it met with Paulus's 6th Army east of Kharkov. Over the next week, strung out over more than 200 miles, the 6th Army with 20 divisions, 250,000 men, 500 panzers, 7,000 guns and mortars and 25,000 horses, pushed down towards the Don corridor on Stalingrad. The tremendous distances which these divisions had to cover could only be achieved by long foot marches but it appeared to be going well.

On 3 July, Hitler left his headquarters for a brief visit to Von Bock's field headquarters in Poltava. On his return flight back to Rastenburg he had given Von Bock permission to capture the strategic city of Voronezh, but categorically ordered him not be drawn into protracted urban fighting and reiterated that under no circumstances did he want another Moscow or Leningrad on his hands.

Three days later, he received reports that Voronezh was captured, but still Hitler held his breath. As he paced his bunker he was told that Bock's units had found themselves inexplicably engaged in a series of heavy street battles, and for two days tried fanatically to hold the city. Seething with anger, Hitler could not believe what had happened. He was so incensed with Bock's negligence that he announced he would relieve him of his command forthwith. Although he admitted that Bock had proven himself as an adequate Eastern Front commander he could not work with generals that were unable follow his directives to the letter.

As Bock headed into retirement, Hitler told his staff to begin packing as the headquarters was being transferred from East Prussia to a forward Eastern Front headquarters in the Ukraine. A week later, on 16 July at 8.15 am his entire staff left the Wolf's Lair and flew in sixteen planes to the new installation, which was situated six miles north of Vinnitsa, just east of the Vinnitsa/Shitomir road.

Inside the dull compound there was an array of wooden huts, very different from the concrete bunkers at the Wolf's Lair. There were no trees, no hills, simply an endless terrain of nothingness. Hitler and his staff hated the place and for the next three months they were compelled to live there. Each evening everyone had to swallow anti-malaria tablets. At night it was very cold inside the log cabins, whilst during the day it was hot and stuffy. Here at Werewolf, Hitler watched Operation Blue unfold. He was optimistic that his forces would soon capture Stalingrad. For the soldiers of the 6th and 4th Armies, whose task it was to take the city, the name Stalingrad bore no real significance, other than it was a city that marked the end point of a very costly summer offensive. To Hitler, however, Stalingrad held more significance. He regarded the city as an 'incubator' of Bolshevism, and despised it as the place where in 1918 Stalin, Budenny, Timoshenko and Voroshilov had defied Trotsky over his policy of war against the Whites, which eventually saw Stalin rise to power.

Hitler was confident of taking the city, but the Russians were equally determined to defend it at all costs. For the Soviets, the time had come for every comrade and citizen to prevent the hated enemy from completing any more ambitious plans in the east. Already millions of soldiers and civilians had perished, and although the Russians had suffered the highest casualties, their devotion to the Motherland and their determination and courage to halt the German crusade continued with fanatical violence. Thus, by late August 1942, with news of German forces on the Don poised to strike across to the west bank of the Volga, the Russians began frantically making preparations not to evacuate the area, but to defend their beloved city.

By 22 August, news reached Werewolf that soldiers of the 6th Army had completed the pontoon bridges across the Don. Tanks, halftracks, self-propelled assault guns, dozens of trucks and reconnaissance vehicles from General Hube's 16th Panzer Division rattled remorselessly across the broad expanse of water onto the east bank. Early the following morning, Count von Strachwitz's *Abteilung* of the 2nd Panzer Regiment, reinforced with panzergrenadier companies, advanced forward from the Don towards the Volga. As they drove eastwards, churning up huge dust clouds, panzer crews could be seen standing fearlessly in their turrets waving their companies forward across the hot and dusty steppe. For these men of the 6th Army it was an historic moment, one their Führer would be proud of.

During the daily war conference Hitler's health once again worsened, and in turn markedly affected his relationship with everybody, most of all his generals. By August, as the 6th Army prepared to attack the outskirts of Stalingrad Hitler was convinced that he could no longer trust his generals. He had been ill-advised, lied to by commanders in the field and deceived by those at his headquarters. His suspicions grew each day and eventually at the conferences he would rarely listen to advice, never to criticism. His growing hatred for the General Staff, coupled with the summer heat, saw him make decisions hastily, especially in one of his raging arguments. His conviction that he was surrounded by traitors escalated as further setbacks on the Eastern Front emerged. Gradually, through the rest of the summer he began to convince himself that his generals were to blame for all the military disappointments and various withdrawals on the Eastern Front.

In early September, after a huge argument with Jodl, Hitler was determined that never again would his orders be disputed or deflected at the conferences. In future all briefing conferences would now take place in his hut. A team of *Reichstag* Stenographers were immediately flown out from Berlin to Vinnitsa to record every word that was spoken during the conferences. The atmosphere at these meetings was uncomfortable, to say the least. No one initiated conversation, but waited anxiously. Hitler would rarely look any of his staff officers in the eye and did not shake hands with them. He would greet them with an icy stare and would conduct the conference in a curt and detached manner.

The stenographers recorded the discussions during these conferences, under the supervision of Martin Bormann. Their records could amount to as much as 500 pages in a single day. Every page was meticulouslyly checked by Hitler's adjutants, and then filed away in secrecy.

In October, the headquarters staff noticed that Hitler once more seemed to be more relaxed and optimistic. The weather at Werewolf was dramatically changing and freezing rain would soon bring snow. Fearing winter in the depths of the Ukraine, Hitler announced over dinner that he intended leaving Vinnitsa for the Wolf's Lair. During the last week of October a memorandum was circulated at the headquarters, instructing the staff of Security Zone I and II, and the field echelon of the OKH quartered nearby in to the town of Vinnitsa, to begin packing for departure.

On 1 November, the entire headquarters returned to Wolf's Lair. War diarist Greiner found it increasingly unpleasant:

> It's horrid here in this dirty green, gloomy, airless forest encampment. It's permanently swathed in fog, it has an exceptionally nasty dining room that couldn't compete with even the ugliest village pub, it has hideous bunkers and barracks that are either overheated or freezing. What's worse is the way things are turning out, there are endless differences of opinion.[15]

Over the last seven months the installation had undergone another major reconstruction. This time more wooden hutments had been erected, which were later covered with brick walls and concrete ceilings to protect them against enemy bombs. Many other buildings too were protected in the same way, including the Navy liaison offices, a second officer's mess, Jodl's offices, Göring's offices, the cinema, the wooden annexes to the *Führerbunker*, the *Keitelbunker*, and the army personnel office. The new tea house that was built adjacent to and east of Kasino I was another very important building that received additional protection. North of Otto Dietrich's bunker/office No.1, stood a very heavily built guest bunker, No.15, for VIP visitors. In order to increase space and additional safety for the *SS-Begleitkommando*, officers of the RSD and his servants, several barracks and bunkers were completed. This included the completion of a sauna. North of the guest bunker, a well guarded barracks-type building was erected. A high fence topped with barbed wire was then added and surrounded the new barracks. Inside this compound were the newly housed stenographers. The building was heavily guarded and no one was allowed in this fenced area except those transcribing what had been said at the military conferences. In one of the larger rooms thousands of transcribed short hand notes were held in boxes and dated. If any discrepancies were ever to arise during the military conferences Hitler and the OKW staff were able to support their position by referring to the recorded discussions that were now held under lock and key in the stenographer barracks.

South of the headquarters, through the western gate into Security Zone II, a number of other buildings were constructed, including one for foreign minister von Ribbentrop's liaison man, one that had been originally assigned to Dr Todt, now Albert Speer, two for the Navy High Command liaison office, and one for the Luftwaffe High Command liaison office; their respective command staffs also had their own liaison officers here.

On 2 November, Hitler spoke at length about another theatre of war that Germany were bitterly contesting, North Africa. That evening, the Wolf's Lair received word that Field Marshal Erwin Rommel was requesting permission to withdraw from El Alamein. By early November, Rommel had lost nearly 12,000 men and 350 panzers. Only a handful of tanks were now at his disposal. With his forces now fighting for survival, he decided to send an urgent message to Rastenburg. That same evening, Hitler duly dispatched a reply telling the 'Desert Fox' that he must not under any circumstances fall back one inch. His troops must, as they had done on the Eastern Front, 'triumph or die'. Yet, during the early hours of the morning a lengthy daily report announcing that Rommel would withdraw from El Alamein arrived by teletype. The night duty officer quickly jotted down the report, but failed to declare that Rommel was actually retreating, thinking that the message was not important enough to disturb the Führer until later that morning. When Hitler awoke at 9.00 am, his adjutant handed him the report over at his bunker. Unsurprisingly, when Hitler read the report he became purple with rage and began shouting, accusing some of his staff officers of conspiring against him. He immediately suspected that OKW had intentionally withheld vital information from him, and had forced Rommel to withdraw. He irritably ordered the night duty officer to be arrested forthwith and marched over to the *Führerbunker* under armed escort. The young, nervous duty officer was then stood in front of Hitler and made accountable for his actions. Broken and drained the duty officer was reduced to the ranks and then marched out of the headquarters to a Detention Battalion. Rommel was exonerated for his part, but General Warlimont, who had been sleeping through Rommel's urgent appeals, took the full blame. As a form of punishment he was relieved of his post forthwith.

Warlimont's sudden departure from the Wolf's Lair had come as a bitter disappointment, especially to the officers of his staff, many of whom were angry over Hitler's behaviour. Keitel for one, openly expressed how sorry he was that he was being evicted from OKW. Schmundt too was also deeply upset and even went to see Hitler to try and get him to recognize that Warlimont may have been treated unfairly. Jodl, on the other hand, was quite unmoved and said with blind obedience that the Führer was the supreme law of the land, and what he said everyone must follow.

A few days later, after much deliberating, Hitler too gradually became aware that Warlimont's dismissal had been unwarranted and asked Schmundt to telephone Warlimont, asking him to return to his post at the Wolf's Lair.

Although the report episode had finally been put to rest, in North Africa the situation had gone from bad to worse, with Rommel continuing to retreat across the blistering desert. Though Hitler had finally approved the decision to withdraw, he felt that the Field Marshal had become increasingly pessimistic, and like so many of his commanders, had completely lost his nerve. He told some of his more intimate staff that if it were not for the regrettable succession of events that had transpired, which had prevented him from intervening in time, defeat in Africa would never have begun.

To add to the problems in North Africa, a shocking intelligence report arrived at the headquarters on 7 November. A huge fleet of enemy ships had entered the Mediterranean and seemed to be bound for the North Africa coast. Over several days intelligence reports had indicated the ships assembling at Gibraltar. Hitler and OKW had assumed that the enemy was bound for Sardinia or Corsica. But to their great surprise, it now looked as if the invasion of Algeria was imminent.

Early that afternoon, with news of the enemy armada still at the forefront of Hitler's mind, he cut short the midday conference and, accompanied by most of his high-ranking staff, left the freezing temperatures of East Prussia bound for Munich. Whilst Hitler was away delivering his anniversary speech to the party's old guard at the *Lowenbraukeller*, back at the Wolf's Lair the General Staff were watching with anxiety one of the fiercest dramas unfolding on the Eastern Front. Within days the burly 47-year-old General Kurt Zeitzler, who had replaced Halder*, telephoned the Berghof and told the Führer of the bitter fighting that was now raging in the smouldering city of Stalingrad.

---

* Halder was dismissed at the Werewolf headquarters on 24 September 1942, after Hitler had blamed the General for the gradual stagnation of the summer offensive. He was replaced by the energetic General Kurt Zietzler, who was considered by Hitler to be his most influential tactical advisor on the Eastern Front.

During the last week of September the 6th Army was still struggling to capture Stalingrad. Inside the city, intense fighting continued as General Zhukov made plans to bring catastrophe to the Germans. On 6 October General Paulus, commander of the 6th Army, temporarily suspended further attacks into the city. His infantry strength had been badly depleted. In the first six weeks since his army moved from the Don, 7,700 soldiers had been killed and 31,000 wounded. Ten per cent of his army was destroyed. In one division, the infantry battalions had an average of three officers, eleven non-commissioned officers, and only 62 men. The ammunition too was dwindling and they were in desperate need of re-supply. In September, the Army had fired off more than 25 million rounds of small arms ammunition, 500,000 anti-tank rounds, and 750,000 artillery shells.

Even Hitler now seemed unsure exactly what to do. Throughout October, the headquarters followed the unmistakable signs of an army being drawn into a protracted urban battle. Reports confirmed that units were pushing forward into the city and resuming their relentless incursion. Through the rubble, the twisted steel of factories, shattered and burnt out wooden houses, cells, sewers, trenches and holes, they fought and tried to survive. During 14 October Paulus sent five divisions against the Barrikady and tractor factory. By midnight, after heavy sustained fighting they had completely surrounded the tractor plant. Losses, however, had been very heavy and during the course of the night some 3,500 wounded were reported. Hour after hour the fighting raged with uncompromising harshness as the German 389th Infantry Division moved deeper into the city. While Zhukov's armies moved into position, the Germans tried their best to gather up enough strength for further fighting in the rubble and burning remains of the doomed city. The difficulties were made worse by the increasing reports of larger Russian formations bearing down on Stalingrad. The situation deteriorated further when Hungarian, Italian, and Rumanian Allied forces began to show signs of crumbling. These ill-equipped, badly trained soldiers had been sent to help bolster their German allies, but after weeks of constant fighting against overwhelming enemy forces many of the soldiers began deserting.

By 23 October, encouraging signs reached the Berghof that the Germans were successfully holding the tractor factory and most of the Barrikady factory, whilst the Red Army held positions inside the Red October Factory. Two days later the Germans captured the centre of Spartakovka, and the 6th Army nearly reached the Volga. German forces now held most of the city, and the remaining part was under merciless fire. These were still tense and critical times at the headquarters. What worried Hitler and his General Staff was the fact that in spite of the situation being dire for the Red Army, they were still fanatically holding out. The Red Army's grim determination to hold at all costs had proven vital for the survival of its men fighting in the ruins of Stalingrad. With the onset of winter fast approaching Hitler was deeply concerned that the tide would turn in their favour.

As the killing continued, the subject of the battle of Stalingrad dominated the situation conferences. Hitler's staff once again noticed a marked changed in his temperament and as a consequence mealtimes with him became rarer. During the conferences as further setbacks were reported on the Eastern Front arguments intensified, Hitler had already openly observed that his generals' nerves were not up to the strain and considered many of them numbskulls.

By mid-November it became increasingly obvious to everyone attending the daily war conferences that Stalingrad was in the process of being encircled. The Red Army was slowly closing its mighty jaws around the city. German troops were swamped by a sea of death and fire. As Russian soldiers surged forward, the tanks and artillery remained in front of them, carpeting the area ahead with shells, rockets and gunfire.

Over the next few days the signs were ominous for Hitler as the Germans struggled against overwhelming numbers. Zhukov had moved some 134 divisions over the Don. Masses of tanks and infantry then spewed across the frozen steppe, whilst hard pressed German forces madly tried to contain them. Frantic calls from Bavaria had already urged Paulus to stand fast until the temporary encirclement had diminished. Hitler was convinced by earlier reports that the Russians were at the point of being bled to death, he still expected the encirclement to last only a matter of days. But as Hitler left Berchtesgaden station during the evening of 23 November, en route to the Wolf's Lair, he received shocking reports that the situation had worsened. To raise Paulus's spirits during one of the darkest, most desperate situations on the Eastern Front thus far, Hitler sent a personal message to him telling the general that he was doing everything he could to help relieve the 6th Army.

As *Amerika* steamed its way through the darkness bound for East Prussia, Hitler and Jodl discussed at length a courageous plan to relieve the beleaguered army at Stalingrad. When Zeitler telephoned Hitler during the train's next halt, he asked for permission to instruct the 6th Army to break out of the city before it was destroyed, but predictably the Führer refused outright.

Later that day the train shunted into Rastenburg station. Through the windows the staff could see that the headquarters were covered in thick snow, adding to the general feeling of despondency. Hitler tried his best to conceal his gloom. When he arrived back in Security Zone I, to his surprise he found Zeitzler already waiting for him outside the *Führerbunker*. He greeted the general with a smile and firmly shook his hand, remarking that he had done everything he could at Stalingrad. As they entered the bunker they spoke at length about the 6th Army. Even though these were the very uneasy times, Hitler still appeared hopeful. Zeitzler, on the other hand, did not share his Führer's confidence and brazenly announced that Paulus's army was doomed if it continued fighting where it was. Hitler lashed out, thumped the desk and cursed the general for his defeatist attitude. Under no circumstances, he yelled, are we moving from the Volga.

Despite rumours that Paulus's army was dying a lingering death, the belief at the Wolf's Lair that the situation was not as desperate as it looked. Already, reserves were on the move preparing for a huge relief offensive directed by Field Marshal Erich Von Manstein. In the weeks to come this relief operation would produce a drama at the headquarters far greater than anything yet experienced. Word in the installation entirely revolved around the only subject anyone wanted to talk about – Stalingrad.

Whilst Hitler and his staff continued to busy themselves with the enormous task of defeating the Soviet Union, Field Marshal Rommel arrived at Security Zone I unannounced and without the Führer's permission. Keitel and Jodl cautiously greeted the Field Marshal and asked him why he had come to the Wolf's Lair without being invited. By five that evening the 'desert fox' was called into the conference room. Hitler was clearly perturbed at Rommel's appearance, especially when he considered that North Africa was a relatively quiet theatre. Grim-faced and hardly able to retain his composure, he listened irritably as Rommel went on about the dire situation in the desert and the problems of the Italian supply line. Pacing the conference room, Hitler did not believe the extent of the problems in North Africa, but reluctantly assured the field marshal that he would send out shipments of supplies. A drained Rommel was then ushered out of the conference room and escorted to the gates of the compound with strict orders to get the Italians to speed up supplies.

In the days that followed, focus was reverted to the Eastern Front. At the map room, Hitler was seen pouring over the map table for hours on end. With a magnifying glass in one hand and colour pencils in the other he scrutinized the red arrows that were deluging the Eastern Front. By the end of November the Russian encirclement of Stalingrad was finally completed. The Red Army had won a great victory in the bend of the Don and had cast out a gigantic envelopment around more than 250,000 German troops between the Don and Stalingrad. Inside the city, the physical condition of the once glorious 6th Army that had steamrolled into Russia seventeen months earlier were now a force fighting for survival. A combination of an inadequate diet, the bitter cold and dwindling mail from loved ones at home, had resulted in an acute decline in morale. Paulus was aware that if his army was to be saved, it would have to be done soon. Tension gripped the headquarters as Hitler and staff worked out a relief operation. To save the 6th Army from complete destruction Manstein was given the task of leading the relief operation, codenamed 'Winter Storm'. The plans seemed impressive, but as each day ominously dragged on towards Manstein's launch date, Winter Storm grew less promising. It was certain that if Manstein failed in his relief effort, then the 6th Army would perish in the fiery cauldron of Stalingrad.

Whilst Paulus did what he could to alleviate the terrible conditions inside Stalingrad, news reached the Wolf's Lair that Manstein's relief attack had begun in earnest in the grey pre-dawn light on 12 December. Winter Storm was spearheaded by General Kirchner's LVII Panzer Corps, consisting of the 6th Panzer Division, which was bolstered by some 160 tanks and 40 self-propelled guns, and the mauled 23rd Panzer Division. Protecting the Panzer corps flanks were Rumanian troops and two weak cavalry divisions. OKW positively predicted that the enemy's tank strength had been strongly reduced and success was inevitable. Hitler seemed more cautious and did not want to appear overly confident as he had done about Stalingrad previously.

At the map room they watched in great suspense as Manstein's force pushed across the frozen plains bound for Stalingrad. During the first few uneasy days of the attack the panzers steadily rolled forward, making good progress over the light snow. Despite this auspicious beginning Manstein's forces were up against resilient opponents. On the second day of the operation the LVII Panzer Corps reached the Aksay River and captured the bridge at Zalevskiy. With heavy Luftwaffe support the advance progressed, but Manstein's forces still had another 45 miles to cover before it reached the pocket. On 17 December the LVII Panzer Corps was increased to three divisions by the arrival of the 17th Panzer Division. With this added strength Kirchner pushed his forces hard across the snow, fighting bitterly as they advanced. Around the town of Kumsky, halfway between the Aksay and Mishkova Rivers, the corps became bogged down in a morass of heavy, protracted fighting against two strong Russian mechanized corps and two tank brigades. It seemed that Manstein's objective to reach the *kessel* to relieve Paulus at Stalingrad was slowly slipping from his grasp. On 18 December, with the cream of his armour burning and his troops fighting to break through what became known as the Aksay Line, the Field Marshal wearily sent a message to Zeitzler requesting immediate steps to initiate the breakout of the 6th Army towards the 4th Army.

At the Wolf's Lair the tension had become so acute that Hitler's health once more changed for the worse. On 17 December, during an important evening conference he suddenly felt weak and dizzy, and could not go on. Morell was immediately called for.

Next day, the Italian foreign minister, Count Galeazzo Cianon arrived at the Wolf's Lair and was met with a frosty atmosphere. Hitler had blamed the Italians for not holding out at Stalingrad and greeted the minister caustically. The visit was made worse when the Count mentioned at the tea house that Mussolini was considering reaching a political settlement with Russia. Hitler bluntly told the minister that there would be no settlement with the Soviets. It was inconceivable, he said, that the Duce even entertained such a proposal for a second when there had already been so much bloodshed. As the Italian party left the Wolf's Lair, a member of the entourage enquired if the Italian forces fighting north-west of Stalingrad had suffered significant losses. An OKW staff officer replied that the troops had not stopped running.

Out in the field, the Italian front had indeed deteriorated and many of its troops were reported to have abandoned their positions. Manstein was frustrated by Germany's allies and telephoned the Wolf's Lair requesting permission for Paulus to break out. Zeitzler approved the request, but Hitler remained resolute, firm in his belief that if the 6th Army pulled out it would jeopardize the entire southern front. The following afternoon, 19 December, the headquarters received another urgent radio appeal from Manstein for permission to break out the 6th Army. During the situation conference that day, Hitler's commanders also voiced their concerns, but despite the noisy consternation of his grumbling commanders, he was adamant that Paulus must stand fast if it meant to the death. Manstein pleaded with Hitler but his efforts were in vain. On 21 December Manstein reported to Hitler that the 4th Panzer Army had advanced to within 30 miles of Stalingrad, but that the resistance from the enemy was so great it could make no more progress. There was also no more fuel for the vehicles and without adequate supplies they were doomed to failure. Hitler had initially been encouraged by the success of the 4th Panzer and had ordered the SS Panzergrenadier Division

Wiking to be transferred from Army Group A to support the Army's drive to Stalingrad, but it was already too late.

Over the next few days leading to Christmas, uneasiness beset the headquarters. No one could relax. Hitler postponed retiring to bed longer every night, deeply concerned that without his leadership Stalingrad might fall. During the daily war conference Hitler was more agitated and this consequently led to arguments with his commanders. Reports only reinforced his worse fears that the 6th Army was on the point of collapse. On Christmas Eve, under merciless Russian attack OKH ordered the 4th Panzer Army to withdraw behind the Aksay River. As German units evacuated the area east of the river, more Russian reinforcements poured across the Volga, both fresh infantry and new tanks, and replaced the exhausted units holding the foothills on the western banks. From their well fortified positions, the Russians continued to use a variety of weaponry to attack German soldiers trapped inside the pocket. Between 22 November and 23 December the 6th Army alone had lost some 28,000 men.

The army reported just before Christmas that the remaining strength inside the pocket was 246,000, including 13,000 Rumanians, 19,300 Russian auxiliaries, and 6,000 wounded. Though the total strength appeared impressive, many of the soldiers were in poor shape and lacked sufficient weapons and ammunition. The combat effectiveness of the troops was further reduced by exhaustion and exposure. Those soldiers that were still fit enough to fight were often frustrated by bad weather. Between the Don and Volga rivers the weather varied considerably. Driving rain, thick snow, and fog perpetually delayed operations.

On Christmas Eve, Manstein brought only despondent news from the front when he radioed the Wolf's Lair that evening. The Field Marshal's blunt revelation that all seemed lost echoed around the headquarters and confirmed Hitler's worst fears of how desperate the situation was at Stalingrad. After Christmas, Hitler was once more warned about the appalling cost of life, but he told Manstein he believed that the 6th Army was safe inside its 'fortress', and could hold out until the spring of 1943. He had ordered Göring to increase the air supply to at least 300 tons a day, believing that this would be sufficient for the 6th Army to survive. But the situation was far worse than Hitler could have ever imagined. His 6th Army was slowly being starved to death. The *kessel* had become littered with thousands of dead, and those stilling holding out were edging towards total obliteration.

On 27 December, Zeitzler arrived unannounced at the headquarters and requested urgently to see the Führer in his private bunker. After being given authorization to enter Security Zone I, the General was escorted by an

RSD guard to the *Führerbunker*, which was now being guarded night and day by the *SS-Begleit-Kommando*. Showing his official pass he was granted access to the bunker and then was then escorted by one of Hitler's adjutants to the Führer's room. In the corner of the room a gramophone was playing a record of Beethoven with Hitler sitting in a soft chair listening. During their conversation the General told Hitler in no uncertain terms of the looming disaster in the Caucasus. He told the Führer blatantly that if he did not order the withdrawal from the Caucasus front forthwith he would have another Stalingrad on his hands. At first Hitler sat quietly and digested the words, and then told Zeitzler to order the withdrawal. But once the General had left, Hitler regretted what he had said and immediately telephoned the general's staff headquarters to try and prevent Zeitzler from executing his order. After numerous attempts to speak to the General he finally came to the telephone, but it was already too late, the order had been issued. As Hitler put down the receiver he was well aware of the consequences that now were beginning to unfold. A general withdrawal from the Soviet Union now seemed inevitable.

In the remaining days of 1942, the stress of the Russian campaign was causing Hitler considerable health problems and ageing him significantly. Dr Morell was seen regularly walking over to the *Führerbunker* to increase Hitler's medication and injections, which frequently included sedatives. His staff tried what they could to relieve him of the constant worries, but generally failed to bring him out of his depression.

During the last conferences held at the end of the year, Hitler had to listen to how the Russians had brilliantly executed their plans of sealing the fate of the 6th Army and breaking up Manstein's attempt to reach the trapped forces. The original success of the battle was mainly attributed to Soviet armour, and not the infantry. In many of the clashes with German forces, it was reported that when the odds were even, Russian troops showed themselves to be distinctly inferior. In fact, although the 6th Army was now dying a lingering death from starvation and exhaustion, its force still processed small advantages against their enemy. One of the main advantages was that in and around Stalingrad, the *kessel* was heavily built up and troops had some shelter. This meant that the chance of survival was far greater than if it had to defend the flat and often treeless steppe between the Don and Volga Rivers. As a consequence, the Soviets did not have the crushing effects that were initially expected, and during the fighting inside the city it regularly lost momentum. The results were often catastrophic, with many thousands of soldiers being killed or wounded. It seemed that the Russians too were paying a very high price in blood for Stalingrad.

Hitler saw the high casualty rate among the Red Army as a glimmer of hope. In front of his intimate staff he even began speaking of turning failure into victory, and optimistically bragged to his secretaries that in 1943, he intended to go on the offensive, in spite of the inevitable disaster looming at Stalingrad.

Chapter IV

Lost Victories

The New Year at the Wolf's Lair opened with reports of a series of well planned withdrawals from the Caucasus. Only in Stalingrad and in the first days of retreat to the Donets did the German Army incur losses of any real significance. Hitler told his staff that he firmly believed that the retreats marked the beginning of the end to the terrible setbacks on the Eastern Front and hoped that victory could still be attained.

During these first worrying weeks of January 1943, reports of the declining situation were still emanating from within Stalingrad. The Red Army pushed ever closer to Stalingrad from the west and bit by bit they captured and destroyed hundreds of pillboxes and other German strong points. During the first half of the month the headquarters received news that some 1,260 German pillboxes and fortified dugouts, including 75 heavily defended observation posts and 317 gun emplacements, had been destroyed. They had also captured or destroyed approximately 400 aircraft, 6,600 tanks and 16,000 trucks. Twenty-five thousand German troops had been killed and several thousand prisoners taken, many of whom were Rumanians. It seemed the Red Army was unstoppable and it was only a matter of time before the 6th Army was completely destroyed. Hitler hoped that Göring's deputy, Field Marshal Erhard Milch, would be able to supply Stalingrad from the air in an effort to avert the impending catastrophe.

During the days that followed the headquarters nervously watched as Milch tried to send adequate air supplies to the besieged troops of the 6th Army. At first there seemed a glimmer of hope, but it soon became apparent that Milch could do little better than the Reich Marshal. Eventually he admitted his mission was impossible. As a consequence of this failure

Hitler's anger and recrimination escalated during the war conferences. The mood at the headquarters was depressing. Hitler once again hardly ventured outside his bunker, preferring to hide himself away and brood over maps, or pour scorn on his military staff. His bitterness and disappointment was so apparent that he would only acknowledge some of his less popular generals with a gimlet stare. Still no one ate their meals with him at one common table, and the small group of stenographers was now permanently assigned among the staff, endlessly scribbling as they conferred.

By 20 January, with the expectation in the air of a disaster approaching, the Wolf's Lair received a frantic message from Paulus requesting permission to break out of the city to avoid total annihilation. Hitler, obstinate as ever, refused. Two days later reports were received that Gumrak, the last airfield, fell as the Russians tore a three-mile gap in the south-western sector. With no fuel and a serious lack of guns and ammunition to repel the Soviets, the 6th Army was unable to close the gap. The following day, the Red Army broke through the western perimeter and leading units penetrated German positions all the way to the tractor works. The Russian drive into Stalingrad was so swift that it actually cut the pocket in two and isolated XI Corps to the north. A weary and exhausted Paulus reported that there were more than 12,000 unattended wounded, many of whom were lying in the streets or inside ruined buildings. Hitler ordered Paulus not to surrender under any circumstances and instructed him that only those capable of fighting would now be fed. The struggle was hopeless and despite stiff resistance in some areas nothing could be done to avert the inevitable destruction of the 6th Army.

On that same day, a Major named Zitzewitz was flown out of Stalingrad to give a report of the situation. He arrived dispirited at the gates of Security Zone I, and was presented to the Führer that same day. 'You have come from a deplorable situation'[16] remarked Hitler as he gripped both of Zitzewitz's hands. Although Hitler had great doubts, he spoke of another relieving drive. The Major, however, was totally unconvinced and thought the idea was absurd. Zitzewitz told the Führer that attacks in undiminished strength were now continually being made against the entire western front, which had been fighting with great losses. In the southern part of Stalingrad, the western front along the city outskirts were being held on to at the western and southern edges, but was on the point of collapse. The Volga and north-eastern fronts were unchanged, but the conditions inside the city were terrible, where 20,000 unattended wounded desperately sought shelter in the ruins. Among the wounded were many starving and frostbitten men and stragglers, often without weapons, which had been lost during the battle. Heavy artillery was pouring a storm of fire on those troops that were holding out. Along the outskirts of the city in the southern part of Stalingrad a last-ditch resistance was being offered, he said, under the courageous leadership of their generals and gallant officers. It was possible, he concluded, that the tractor works could hold out a little longer. Hitler was clearly moved by the report and spoke emotionally of the death throes of the 6th Army, but still, he said, he could not be moved in his resolve. The battle of Stalingrad must continue at all and any costs.

During the evening conference, Hitler had to listen to more depressing reports from Stalingrad. Paulus's army was now broken into two pockets and conditions were appalling. Those soldiers that no longer had the energy and willpower to fight, sought shelter in the dank cellars and basements of the ruined buildings. Here, in unimaginable horror and torment, the sick, frostbitten, wounded and dying soldiers lay packed together. Many of them had dysentery, tetanus, spotted fever, typhus, pneumonia or gangrene. Up above, across the fire-raked devastation, the rest of the 6th Army was slowly being incinerated in the inferno. Paulus himself was now a General enervated with dysentery, and it was worryingly reported that he was close to suffering a nervous breakdown. His headquarters was now situated in the ruins of a large department store in Red Square, defended by what was left of General Hartmann's 71st Infantry Division.

Shuffling back through the snow to his bunker, accompanied by one of his adjutants, Hitler appeared burdened by deep troubles. For long periods he could be seen sitting in his bunker staring at the map, watching the red arrows of the Soviet Army's offensive edge ever closer, swamping the beleaguered city. Disaster was imminent, but during the following conferences held in late January his war staff noticed that the Führer appeared more optimistic about the future. He appeared to have written off the 6th Army but assured his generals that out of the catastrophe a new land would thrive because of the sacrifices of the fallen. It was this ardent belief, he said, that had given Paulus the inspiration to obey his orders to the letter. None of the generals dared mention that Paulus had been given no choice in the matter, and was compelled to fight to the death inside the doomed city. Nevertheless, on 30 January Paulus radioed the Wolf's Lair after receiving a message from the Führer, and gave a dignified response to his admiration of the 6th Army.

As Paulus prepared to arm himself for his last battle, Hitler decided to shower promotions on the 6th Army's senior officers. Paulus was promoted to Field-Marshal, Hitler knowing very well that no German soldier of that rank had ever surrendered. In front of his General Staff Hitler said that he had finally found a brave gentleman that would keep the last bullet for himself, and would never capitulate to the Soviets. Unaware of his Führer's expectation that he either die fighting or commit suicide before surrendering to the Russians, the newly decorated Field-Marshal emphasized his burning allegiance to Hitler, told him that a swastika still fluttered over the city and that out of the deplorable situation Germany would still be victorious.

January 30 was a nerve wracking day for all those that attended the war conference. It was now a foregone conclusion among all the war staff, including Hitler, that Stalingrad was lost. Reports received from Paulus's command were now greeted as a matter of procedure, rather than there being any attempt to avert the inevitable outcome. During that day it was reported that fighting intensified as Red Army forces began overwhelming the last German defensive positions. The 76th Infantry Division was surrounded and forced to surrender. Near the railway station number 1, the headquarters of the XIV Panzer Corps was also compelled to capitulate. In the northern pocket, Russian T-34s had smashed their way through and decimated hundreds of German troops. Within a matter of hours the command bunkers of the VIII and LI corps were captured. Generals Sydlitz, Heitz and five others reluctantly surrendered. The Russians then attacked the 71st Infantry and during the vicious street fighting General Hartmann was killed. Soviet troops were also closing in on Paulus's command post.

The following day the headquarters held their breath as the last parts of the battle were being fought out. Whilst Hitler was still sleeping it had been reported that at 6.15 am, the radio operator in Paulus's headquarters had been trying to send out a frantic message, but the radio went dead. There was now no more communication with Paulus's command post. Whilst the Wolf's Lair tried its best to monitor the battle, Hitler busied himself with plans of how to deal with the aftermath.

On the first day of February at 2.30 am, Hitler finally forced himself to retire to bed following a day of high drama. Shortly afterwards he was disturbed with word from Moscow; Paulus had discredited himself by surrendering, as had 105,000 troops, eleven German and five Rumanian Generals. Hitler quickly got dressed and called for Keitel and Jodl to meet him at the map room. In front of his OKW commanders he exploded with indignation and heaped abuse on the Field-Marshal for surrendering. News of the capitulation soon spread throughout the shocked headquarters. Alongside the astonishment was an underlying fear that perhaps Stalingrad marked the end of the German military initiative in the East. Hitler was aware that he had lost an army and a very important campaign. Both the banks of the Don and the Volga were now littered with the dead and the once vaunted 6th Army had been destroyed. Although Hitler insisted that the 6th Army had provided a valuable service by tying down almost 750,000 enemy troops, the loss of the campaign was immense. His forces were now faced with a relentlessly growing and improving Red Army.

At the midday conference, Zeitzler and other staff members could not believe that the 6th Army had been totally destroyed. Privately, Hitler felt more than ever that he was fighting the War alone. Yet, as Commander-in-Chief of the Army he chose to accept the blame of the loss of the city and made no attempt at this stage to find a scapegoat for his grave military error. He did, however, contemplate attributing some of the blame to Göring, by saying that he had been given misleading information on the Luftwaffe's capabilities, but concluded that it would serve no purpose to make him accountable.

After the disaster at Stalingrad, Göring's popularity at the Wolf's Lair deteriorated. The Reich Marshal, meanwhile, judged the headquarters very harshly. He found a number of Hitler's staff officers arrogant and only had negative words to say about Jodl who had begun to tell jokes about Hitler. He criticized the working methods of many of the headquarters staff and thought it ludicrous that the stenographers were always present during staff conferences and taking down every word. Göring considered Schmundt to be the only honest and trustworthy personality in Security Zone I.

For the next days and weeks there was a general realization at the war conferences that the tide of the War had really turned against Germany. The weather did nothing to lessen the depression they felt, especially Hitler, who now seemed a constant picture of gloom. Those who visited the Wolf's Lair, who had not seen the Führer for many months, found a changed man. General Heinz Guderian was shocked by his appearance:

> His manner was less assured than it had been and his speech hesitant. His left hand trembled, his back was bent, his gaze was fixed, his eyes protruded but lacked their former lustre, and his cheeks were flecked with red. He easily lost his composure, and was prone to angry outbursts and ill-considered decisions in consequence.[17]

Hitler's physical and mental state clearly showed signs of alteration; normally he would spend time recuperating at his Berghof mountain retreat, but he repeatedly said he did not have the time. With the increasing demands made on him by the War he was often seized by deep moods of depression. Day after day he sat, worrying, in his badly ventilated bunker and refused to read military reports that contradicted the picture that he wanted to form in his own mind. In the depths of his dejection, attendance at military briefing was kept to only a handful of staff officers. He managed to control his temper within his intimate circle but remained uncharacteristically distant and hesitant in conversation. According to Fraulein Schroder, after Stalingrad

> Hitler would no longer listen to music any more, and every evening we had to listen to his monologues instead. But his table talk was by now as overplayed as his gramophone record ... World affairs and events at the front was never mentioned: everything to do with the War was taboo.[18]

For this reason Hitler stopped inviting guests at mealtimes, preferring to eat alone or with his secretaries, who were under strict instruction not to mention the War. Even during his depression Hitler still treated his secretaries and adjutants politely. This was the side of the Führer that the generals never saw. They did not see him like some of the staff at the headquarters, courteous with the secretaries, affable with the servants and gregarious with the chauffeurs. In their eyes, Hitler was bad tempered and arrogant. At the conferences they felt extremely constrained in his presence and that they could not speak their mind. Stenographer Thot, however, found Hitler quite affable, he had even asked the stenographers if they wanted an electric bowl fire to warm their places at the table because the room was very cold.

Hitler's life at the headquarters, and everyone else's, continued to echo the bleakness of the surroundings. The sense of isolation in the gloom of the installation was felt by most visitors to be oppressive. The most dominant impression of life at the Wolf's Lair during those first freezing months of 1943, was one of soul-destroying boredom, punctuated by military drama and Hitler's unpredictable rages.

Goebbels, who visited Hitler, was shocked by his appearance and unhealthy existence. He noted in his diary that the Führer had become a recluse and never left his bunker for fresh air. He added that he never relaxed, but just sat brooding. Life at the Wolf's Lair, he concluded, was undoubtedly having a very depressing effect on Hitler.

Under the combined pressures of such a life, Hitler's increasing hours of work became monotonously regular. Awakened daily about noon, all his engagements consisted of a series of appointments with generals, politicians, adjutants, doctors and secretaries, relieved only by a meal, and a very occasional stroll with his Alsatian bitch, Blondi, to which he had become very attached. Usually he rested in the late afternoon in his bunker, resuming with his last war conference in the evening, which sometimes was followed with tea in the company of his secretaries or other close associates. By about four in the morning he would depart to his bunker for bed. The strain was huge, yet he was still able to maintain a very tight hold on all the staff that worked and lived at the headquarters.

During the first months of 1943, Hitler and his war staff were preoccupied with the reverberations caused by the loss of Stalingrad. For weeks the war conferences were dominated by Hitler's insistence on regaining the military initiative in the East. Although many parts of the Eastern Front remained static, in the south and in the Ukraine the campaign was being decided. By February, the front had moved almost 200 miles in less than three months. But despite the German retreat, the Soviets' first experience of an offensive was proving more difficult than they first envisaged, and they were beginning to falter.

Emboldened by what he considered a significant, dramatic reversal of fortune, during the evening conference on 16 February Hitler announced his decision to go to the front and take over command of Army Group South. He would take just Jodl, Zeitzler, Schmundt, Hewel and Morell with him. By early next morning Hitler's motorcade left the Wolf's Lair for the Rastenburg airfield, bound for the long flight south to Manstein's headquarters. According to Hitler's new private secretary, Gertraud (Traudl) Humps:

> By afternoon the Führer's bunker was deserted. It was strange, the hush that suddenly descended on the whole compound. It was as if the main dynamo of the concern had stopped. This was the first time I sensed how much Hitler's personality acted as a mainspring for all these men – the puppet-master, who help all the marionettes' strings in his hands, had suddenly let them fall.[19]

Traudl Humps was the newest face in the inner circle at the headquarters and was the granddaughter of a general. She was just 22 years old when she first arrived at the Wolf's Lair. She was so nervous the first time she took dictation, that Hitler soothed her, 'as if I was a child'. 'You don't have to get excited' he said, 'I myself will make more mistakes during dictation than you will.'[20] She was summoned again on 3 January. This time the Führer asked if she would like the job of permanent private secretary, 'a job that thousands of young girls would have died for'.[21] It was an exciting and flattering offer, which she accepted without hesitation. She was brought to the Wolf's Lair to replace Gerda Daranowsky. Daranowksy had left a job with Elizabeth Arden to work for Hitler, and now she was marrying a Luftwaffe officer.

Traudl Humps soon became accustomed to this strange new world. With no busy office or fixed working hours, she had plenty of time for leisure, much of which was spent wandering the forests and lakes. She particularly enjoyed watching her new employer play with his dog, Blondi:

> The big dog would jump through hoops, leap over a six-foot wooden wall, climb up a ladder, then beg at the top. When the Führer would notice me, he would come over, shake hands and asked how I was doing.[22]

Hitler's stay at Manstein's headquarters only lasted a couple of days and with the sound of Russian tank fire nearing the headquarters, Hitler decided it was time to leave Zaporozhye for his Ukrainian headquarters, Werewolf. His stay lasted nearly four weeks and on 13 March, as the daytime temperatures rose above freezing for the first time, he left Vinnitsa, never to see the headquarters again. That evening he returned to the Wolf's Lair, after first calling at Kluge's Army Group Centre headquarters in Smolensk.

The next day, his staff found Hitler in good spirits. In front of his commanders he openly remarked that his decision to hold firm in the East had saved the German Army from complete catastrophe. Reports from the front had confirmed that during the last two weeks of February a complete reversal of fortune had gripped the German Army, which was later called by the soldiers that fought in it, the 'Miracle of the Donetz'. South of the city of Kharkov, under converging pressure from General Hoth's two Panzer Corps, the exhausted Russian armies began to disintegrate and retreat in an easterly direction, allowing German forces to recapture the city. The German Army, it seemed, had yet again demonstrated its renowned powers of recovery.

With the Eastern Front more or less paralysed by the thaw, Hitler announced that he had decided to retire for a couple of weeks to the Berghof. On 20 March, Hitler and his headquarters entourage boarded his special train, now secretly renamed *Brandenburg*. It was a clear, mild winter night, and as they left the snow-covered headquarters, Traudl Humps was saddened to leave, yet excited at the prospect of travelling on Hitler's train and seeing his mountain retreat.

Two months later, on 12 May, Hitler and staff left the Berghof briefly to fly back to the Wolf's Lair. The next day, as Hitler began settling down in his bunker to a normal working routine, his Armaments Minister, Albert Speer, along with leaders of the armaments industry, were escorted inside the gates of Security Zone I. They had come to East Prussia to discuss the economic implications of the loss of North Africa. Hitler congratulated Speer for the reorganization of the armaments industry and awarded him the *Doctor Todt Ring*, for his achievements. The following day Hitler appeared in an expansive mood as Speer's new weapons were demonstrated at the headquarters. Afterwards, Hitler, Speer and his officials returned to Security Zone I where they had tea.

For the next fortnight, concern began to grip the headquarters following the dangerous situation left by the defeat in North Africa. On 15 May, after the noon conference, Hitler made a speech to his generals, including Rommel, and outlined in particular the growing military problem in Italy. He categorically insisted that under no circumstances could Germany afford a second front to emerge in Europe. For that reason he was compelled to make sacrifices for its defence by moving much needed troops from the Eastern Front. He even suggested abandoning the new offensive in the East called operation 'Citadel'.

The new offensive that Hitler had been planning was a big gamble. But he remained confident in front of his commanders that he could repeat earlier devastating victories against the Soviet Army. It was at Kursk that the Führer was confronted with a very tempting strategic opportunity that he was convinced could yield him victory. Within the huge salient, measuring some 120 miles wide and 75 miles deep, he had tried to persuade his generals for some weeks that his force could attack from the north and south of the salient in a huge pincer movement and encircle the Red Army. In Hitler's view, the offensive would be the greatest armoured battle ever won on the Eastern Front and would include the bulk of his mighty Panzerwaffe, among them premier Waffen-SS divisions, the elite of his fighting force.

Whilst OKW and OKH busied themselves with plans for Citadel, at 1 pm on 21 May, after a brief treatment session with his personal surgeon Dr Karl Brandt, Hitler once more left his headquarters bound for his mountain retreat. Although he remained optimistic in front of his staff, uncertainty still gnawed at his every waking moment, especially about Italy.

On 1 July, after spending almost six weeks at the Berghof, Hitler and staff were transferred back to East Prussia. Citadel was now in the forefront of his mind. When they arrived at the Wolf's Lair the air was unusually cold for the time of the year, and this added to the general despondency. That same evening, Hitler addressed his Citadel commanders, gathered at Zeitzler's OKH headquarters. In clear and ringing tones, Hitler told them 'I intend to fix the starting date of Citadel for the 5th of July.' He made it known from the outset that the operation had limited objectives. He concluded that he did not want his forces becoming embroiled, as they had done at Stalingrad, in a drawn-out, bitter battle.

Over the next few days high drama gripped the Wolf's Lair as Citadel was poised to begin. Uncertainly about the battle continued to preoccupy Hitler, and many of his staff noticed that he had become very pale and withdrawn. During the nights Hitler would be seen over at the map room trying to deduce where the heaviest fighting would take place. With virtually no sleep and one conference after another, his health had again deteriorated, but there was no time for rest. On the eve of the attack the headquarters was charged with apprehension. All night Hitler was seen pacing the corridors and rooms of his bunker, constantly talking about the coming battle in the East. His anxieties had become so bad that he told his adjutant that he decided to go to bed much earlier than usual, but could not sleep.

Early next morning, whilst Hitler lay on his bunk staring up at the grey, bare concrete ceiling of his bunker, 700 miles away to the east, Citadel had begun in earnest. During the early morning of 5 July, German forces unleashed one of their largest artillery bombardments of the War. In fact, the bombardment was so intense that in one hour the Germans had hurled more shells than they had used in both Poland and the Western Campaign put together. Once the bombardment had subsided German ground forces were ordered forward into action. Their objective was to break through the Kursk-Orel highway and railway and then drive southwards to Kursk. By daybreak, Hitler received the first reports confirming that his forces had moved forward and an immense, bloody battle had ensued. Over the next few days Hitler repeatedly telephoned Zeitzler, anxious to find out the latest news of the battle. Early on the 6th, Morell went to see Hitler; he wrote in his diary: 'Injections as always ... slept only three hours because of his nervousness'.[23] For the next few days Citadel remained OKW's constant preoccupation.

At Kursk, German troops tried their best to push forward under relentless Russian fire. In 9th Army, XIII Army Corps, which was by far the strongest in both men and anti-tank guns, faced the strongest defensive positions in the entire salient and was used as a battering ram against the enemy. But as with all other sectors of the front, at Kursk, the Red Army, despite continuing to incur huge losses in both men and weaponry, prevented the XIII Army Corps and the rest of the forces in 9th Army from achieving their objectives. The Russians, it was confirmed, were continually strengthening their defences through reinforcement, skilfully deploying mobile armour and anti-tank reserves to compensate for the high losses.

Within 24 hours of the initial attack, the 9th Army's 25-mile front had been reduced to 20 miles. By 7 July this dropped to around 8 miles wide, and the following day, to less than 1 mile. Not only had the front shrunk, but the depth of the German attack had been significantly reduced. In the south of the salient, Hitler received more encouraging reports that relatively good progress was being achieved. But as in the north, attack frontages and penetration depth were reduced as the attack proceeded. Consequently, within three days the front had been reduced from 16 to 1½ miles. Yet again the Russians had held their positions to the last man. The many thousands of mines and artillery pieces were successful in delaying the German attack and inflicting appalling losses. In fact, across the threatened sectors of the front where German forces seemed to penetrate areas more deeply, the Russians had quickly brought up additional stocks of mines. According to an OKH report, it was estimated that some 90,000 of these mines alone were laid during the battle by small, mobile groups of engineers at night. Within five days of heavy fighting, many German units had lost immeasurable amounts of men and equipment. The elite Grossdeutschland Division for instance, which began the battle with 118 tanks, only had 3 Tigers, 6 Panthers, and 11 Pz.Kpfw.IIIs and IV tanks left operational. The XLVIII Panzer Corps reported 38 Panthers operational with 131 awaiting repair, out of the 200 it started with on 5 July.

By 12 July, the Red Army had ground down the German Army at Kursk and thrown its offensive timetable off schedule. Hitler was clearly disturbed by the setback and told his generals that he was thinking of calling off Citadel altogether. The next day, as further news from Kursk brought increasing gloom to the *Führerbunker*, Hitler summoned both army group commanders, Manstein and Kluge to the Wolf's Lair. He told them that in view of reports of enemy landings on Sicily, where Italians were not even attempting to fight, it was necessary to form new armies in Italy and the western Balkans. These forces, he said, must be found from the Eastern Front, so Citadel had to be stopped. In other words, Hitler knew that if he continued with the offensive, the whole of Army Group Centre would be under threat, if not destroyed.

The Soviets had savagely contested every foot of ground and were finally on an equal footing. The German offensive at Kursk had dealt them a severe battering and ended the largest tank battle in history. It was reported at the Wolf's Lair that the Germans had lost some 30 divisions, including seven Panzer divisions. As many as 40,000 German troops were killed or missing. They had lost a staggering 1,614 of the tanks and self-propelled guns that were committed to action. The Red Army, however, had suffered much greater losses. (The loss figures for Kursk are notoriously difficult to confirm; for the best account, see the book *Zitadelle* by Mark Healy.)

Much to the relief of Hitler, for the time being it seemed stability had once more returned to the Eastern Front as exhausted Red Army forces re-supplied. In spite of the German failure at Kursk, Hitler and OKW clung to the view that fighting there had squeezed all available resources out of the Red Army. They ardently believed that the rest of the summer campaign could be devoted to a series of tactical solutions that could straighten out the front and prepare its defences for the onset of the winter.

In southern Russia it was reported that a number of advanced units of Army Group South had tried their best to hold onto vital areas of ground in order to contain the overly extended front. During the last two weeks of July, Army Group South had a total of 822,000 troops opposing an estimated 1,710,000 Russians. Here in the south, commanders expressed their concerns at the situation conferences that the majority of units were seriously under strength and still further depleted by vehicles constantly being taken out for repair. This undoubtedly left a substantial lack of armour to support the troops on the front lines. As a consequence, Army Group South had been forced to withdraw in order to prevent being cut off through deep enemy breakthroughs and suffer the same fate as that of the 6th Army at Stalingrad. During the last week of July a report was received at the Wolf's Lair that a substantial amount of men and equipment had withdrawn into the Donetz area.

Although Hitler was perturbed by the events on the Eastern Front, he was aware that tactical withdrawals were inevitable. Grudgingly, he accepted the fact that the war in Russia would have to continue throughout 1943, and hoped that fortitude in his generals would prevent a rout.

On 18 July, with Citadel still painfully alive in his mind, he left the Wolf's Lair, boarded his personal FW200 Condor and flew with some of his staff to Berchtesgaden, where he would journey to northern Italy to meet Mussolini.

Within a couple of days he had arrived back at Rastenburg exhausted from all the travelling. He looked deathly white, and the worry on his thin pale face was evidence of the stress he was suffering. Since Stalingrad, never had a month brought such high drama at the headquarters as July 1943. Shut away in his badly ventilated bunker, he brooded over Italy and the worries that Mussolini's own position was gradually slipping away. By 9.30 pm, on 25 July, Hitler was handed a piece of paper from his adjutant telling him that the Duce had resigned. In a conversation with Keitel later that evening, Hitler remarked that the traitor Badoglio had taken over the government. Although Hitler had anticipated the fall of fascism in Italy, the loss of Mussolini sent shock waves through the headquarters.

With the Duce's sudden departure from Government, Hitler summoned his leaders to the Wolf's Lair for an immediate conference. Goebbels, Göring, Ribbentrop, Himmler and Donitz along with several of his staff arrived. Guderian too left the front, and Schmundt was hurriedly ordered back from leave. Speer, however, was already at Rastenburg.

For the next few days, Hitler held a series of war conference with no less than 30 people packed in the hot and stuffy room at one time. During these long drawn out debates, a number of key decisions regarding the axis alliance were worked out. Great emphasis was put on restoring Mussolini's fascist government.

Over the next few days and weeks, whilst German forces tried to hold their lines on the Eastern Front, Hitler and his staff continued devoting much of their time to dealing with the unhappy state of the axis powers. Yet in spite of Hitler's commitment to the Duce, nothing could mask the fact that his alliance with the Italians was slipping from his grasp.

By way of contrast, while the Wolf's Lair was busily preoccupying itself with its strength in the Mediterranean, Stalin had mounted a series of attacks along huge stretches of the Eastern Front. In the middle sector of the Eastern Front, Army Group Centre was trying to desperately hold the Red Army from breaking through their line. But their strength too had been severely weakened by the Citadel offensive and by 5 August, news reached the headquarters that the Soviets had captured Orel. Simultaneous drives along the southern sector of the front saw the Red Army take Kharkov, the most fought-over city in Russia. Soviet troops were then reported to have pressed forward and crossed the Donetz. It was realized during the war conferences that these powerful Red Army drives would soon threaten to envelop General Kleist's Army Group A, which was still bitterly contesting every foot of ground in the Crimea. Manstein immediately telephoned the headquarters requesting additional forces, or that Hitler permit withdrawal.

As a result of the deteriorating situation in the Crimea, Hitler decided to leave the Wolf's Lair on 27 August and fly to the Ukraine to promise Manstein that he would provide whatever divisions he could possibly muster to avert a catastrophe. By early evening his plane was carrying him back to Rastenburg airfield. But the very next day he broke his promise to Manstein as worrying reports that another enemy breakthrough had been made, this time on Army Group Centre.

Already Army Group Centre had been pierced in three places and the whole sector in that part of the Eastern Front began to collapse under the sheer weight of the Red Army. In fact, attacks were so heavy that it actually prompted Kluge to personally make a flying visit to the Wolf's Lair, to try to talk Hitler out of further weakening Army Group Centre. His attempt failed.

A few days later, with still no respite from the Red Army, Kluge made another flying visit, this time with Manstein. Again they pressed Hitler for a decision regarding reinforcements. But following careful consideration, Hitler calmly told both disgruntled generals that still no additional forces could be spared, either from other theatres or from the Northern Army Group. He was, however, willing to allow Manstein to withdraw Hollidt's new 6th Army briefly encircled on the sea of Azov.

By 8 September, with the Eastern Front still in jeopardy, Hitler decided to fly out to Manstein's Ukrainian headquarters again. Whilst he was preparing for his journey he was handed a report saying that advanced Russian units were no less than 30 miles from the Dnieper River, and were sending powerful units towards the city of Kiev.

Hitler's visit to Manstein's headquarters barely lasted 90 minutes. By 12.45 pm he was airborne again, leaving Russian soil forever. He was back at the Wolf's Lair in conference by 5.00 pm. The topic of conversation was momentarily diverted from the drama unfolding in the East to the situation in Italy.

After the conference, anxious and tired, Hitler walked back to his bunker and briefly took a nap in his room. As he lay on his bunk he was disturbed by word that Italy had signed an armistice with the West. Although briefly shaken by the news, he said that he was finally relieved of the uncertainty. With Italy lost he was now worried that public opinion might deteriorate and decided that he should broadcast a speech to the nation.

Late on 10 September from the *Führerbunker*, Hitler, surrounded by Göring, Himmler and some members of his staff, gave a 20-page speech to the nation. Those who joined him at the tea house afterwards said they were truly invigorated by his amazing demonstration of confidence. Despite his waning health, his gift as an orator seemed to have influenced the morale of his closest associates. Those who were actually directing the War however, were not so convinced.

Two days later, on 12 September, spirits in the headquarters were once again raised. Whilst Hitler was having supper with Himmler, he was interrupted by a manservant clutching an urgent telephone message. Mussolini had been found and rescued from a mountain prison by Otto Skorzeny, and had just arrived in Vienna with him. Hitler could hardly contain himself and jumped to his feet at the news; in an instant he telephoned Skorzeny, and told him that he had performed a military feat which would become part of history, saying, 'You have given back my friend Mussolini.'

During the morning of 14 September, Hitler drove to the Rastenburg airstrip to meet the plane bringing the wane and drawn Italian dictator up from Munich. As Mussolini disembarked and stepped onto Prussian soil Hitler warmly embraced him, and for some time they stood hand in hand. Hitler was shocked by the appearance of the Duce who looked sick and unkempt in his dark blue suit. Those that witnessed him step off the plane saw a completely different Mussolini from the once powerful, well groomed image that they had become accustomed to. Privately, everyone was aware that his political days were now over.

During the Duce's brief stay at the Wolf's Lair, Hitler astonished his guest by announcing that he had been seriously considering settling the score over Russia with Stalin. For hours on end he paced up and down the map room, speculating such a compromise with his old arch enemy. Yet, those around him knew that the Führer did not really want peace. Already, too much blood had been spilt on the battlefield to even contemplate such a bold compromise.

In the weeks and months that followed, Hitler and staff increasingly began to discuss the problems of fighting wars on many fronts with dwindling resources. The hard and costly struggle against the Soviets had cost the German war economy dearly, but now an even greater threat began to unfold during the conferences; an Anglo Saxon landing in the West, possibly France. At a conference held on 30 October, Hitler believed that an invasion would come in the spring the following year, and he was certain that it would be in northern France. Both Jodl and Rundstedt supported his views. Hitler then ordered Rundstedt to send a team to plan for a possible second line of defence.

Whilst defensive plans were being drafted in preparation for an Allied invasion of northern France, Hitler once more turned his attention to the East. The summer campaign had already been disastrous for the German Army, and in southern Russian in particular forces had withdrawn 150 miles along a 650-mile front. In spite of Hitler's decree of a 'Scorched Earth

Policy', in which the main roads, railway lines, power stations, farms and factories were to be destroyed, the demolition teams did not have enough time to implement the destruction of the main roads, allowing the Red Army to use them for its main advance.

By the end of October, a feeling of despair prevailed across the entire German Army. Hitler had heard rumours from the front that commanders in the field were depressed at the prospect of enduring a third winter in Russia without any sight of an end to the War. In spite of their dull conviction, the troops still dug deep into the heartlands of Soviet Russia. However, unlike in 1941 and 1942, they had lost the initiative. Slowly and definitely the German soldiers retreated across a bleak and hostile landscape, always outnumbered, constantly low on fuel, ammunition and other desperate supplies. In three months following the defeat at Kursk, Army Group South alone had received some 32,000 replacements, although it suffered more than 130,000 casualties. The equipment situation too continued to decline, especially in Panzer units. In front of his war staff Hitler was well aware that the whole of the German Army in the East were facing a more dangerous and worsening situation than ever before.

As circumstances further deteriorated, Hitler was increasingly seen ridiculing his commanders' tactics. Many of them, he said, had become pessimists as far as reports to him were concerned. He no longer believed anything that was not proven to him and was sceptical about every cable and dispatch that he was handed. When he was given reports that soldiers privately no longer believed in final victory, he immediately blamed his generals for generating despondency among the ranks. Like Julius Caesar, he believed, he had to watch his back. Since 1939, he had been fighting the War with a group of generals that he not only mistrusted, but disliked individually as well. As another winter on the Eastern Front beckoned, he was convinced more than ever that the only way to win the War was to rid himself of what he considered were stale military experts, and surround himself with men like his old party faithful. But for Hitler, imprisoned in a tomb of concrete and wood, there was now no time. Instead he felt compelled to fight the turbulent months ahead with the one tool on which he had to rely on, but was basically opposed to him.

Over the coming months Hitler began to blame his generals for breaking long-distance telephone conversations, and leaks of secret information. He assumed that all the sources had come direct from the Wolf's Lair, and for this reason he ordered the stepping up of all security measures within the headquarters. On 20 September, Schmundt and NSKK-*Gruppenführer* Albert Bormann issued new directives to increase security and secrecy within Security Zone I. A new security restricted zone was created within Security Zone I called Security Zone A. It included the bunkers and annexes of the personal adjutants (No.8), of mess (No.1) and a tea house (No.10), Keitel (No.7), of the Führer (No.11), of Bormann (No.12) and of Hitler's Wehrmacht adjutants office, army personnel (No.13).

In Security Zone A the secrecy of all conferences in the Führer's presence, or near him, was guaranteed by every available means. Hitler insisted that any persons who spoke on matters about which others did not need to know were to be reported to him personally for disciplinary punishment. Only persons who had their offices in Security Zone A or were serving with Hitler directly, were allowed in and were issued with new passes. Day passes could also be issued but only after permission had been given by one of Hitler's military adjutants. As long as he held a valid pass, a visitor entering through the gate was always accompanied by a guard. If anyone was found without a valid pass in Security Zone A, which was almost impossible, he would be immediately arrested, marched out of the installation and thoroughly interrogated.

As for motor vehicles that entered Hitler's restricted zone, it was once again limited to cars of importance such as Reich leaders, Reich ministers and field marshals upwards. Generals travelling in their staff cars were ordered to disembark outside Security Zone A, and would then be escorted by armed guard to the gate, show their valid pass to the guard on gate duty, who would in turn ask what business they had within the Zone, before giving them access. If they required access to the *Führerbunker*, another guard would escort them directly to the bunker who would then hand over the visitor to one of Hitler's adjutants.

Security Zone A was now even more secure than ever before. The three gates at Bormann's, the adjutants', and Keitel's buildings were all guarded by one non-commissioned officer of the FBB and one RSD officer. Inside the compound one RSD officer constantly patrolled the area of Security Zone A, scrutinizing everyone's movements and making sure that the Führer's wishes of increased security and secrecy were adhered to at all times.

On 20 September a security order was issued:

Führer HQ, 20 September 1943

1. Security Zone A is newly created with Security Zone I. The new regulation comes into effect at 1700 on 22 September 1943.

2. The following houses belong with Security Zone A: General Keitel; the Führer's personal adjutants: Kasino I and Tea house, the Führer; Reichsleiter Bormann; Heerespersonalamt etc.

3. Security Zone A has been set up on the basis of an instruction by the Führer. The Führer has ordered: All steps are to be taken to ensure that events, intentions, conversations etc. Held in his presence or that of his immediate circle at FHQ are kept secret. The Führer has ordered that any person who speaks to another person of a matter which is secret and must not be divulged is to be reported to him for disciplinary action. Secrecy and the safety of the Führer's person are the factors behind the creation of Security Zone A.

4. The Führer's orders may bring about stringent measures which mean hardship to this or that party. However, personal wishes must be subordinated to the need for increased security and secrecy.

5. The circle of persons rightfully in Security Zone A are those having duty with the Führer and not the aides. This rule does not apply to those persons resident in Security Zone A.

6. It is most important that visitor traffic in the Security Zone is restricted. However, some visits to Security Zone I command centres for conferences as well as courier traffic are unavoidable and the creation of Security Zone A will serve the purpose of limiting visitor movement.

7. Persons resident in Security Zone A, or resident outside it but whose duties will bring them continually into Security Zone A, will be issued with a long-term pass bearing the holder's photographic likeness. Other long-term passes for Security Zone A will be issued by the HQ commandant only with the approval of the chief adjutant of the Wehrmacht to the Führer or his deputy and in agreement with SS-Obergruppenführer Schaub and his deputy. The passes valid hitherto will be withdrawn.

8. A day pass for Security Zone A may only be issued by the guardroom if previously authorized by a personal or military Adjutant to the Führer. Corresponding requests must be made in good time to permanent Adjutants. No person may enter Security Zone A without a pass, not even in company of another person who holds a valid pass. Only the RSD officials on gate duty are authorized in exceptional cases to admit a person to Security Zone A without a pass; however they must always accompany that person. The official must bring the visitor to his destination to confirm the right of entry. The duplicate pass must then be issued and worn, or the visitor escorted by the RSD official back to the gate. No person must be alone in Security Zone A without a pass. Officials and sentries have instructions that

in the event of such an occurrence, the person concerned is to be directed out of the Security Zone or arrested. The requirements for Security Zone I remain in force as per instructions issued on 9 September 1943.

9. Motor traffic in Security Zone A is to be discouraged as much as possible. Parking in Security Zone O is forbidden. Only the cars of the Reich Minister, Reich leaders and field marshals may enter. These persons and anybody accompanying them must be in the possession of a valid pass and produce it for inspection whenever requested to do so. All other persons must leave their vehicle at the gate, excepting officers resident in Security Zone A and those driving delivery vehicles.

10. Foot traffic to command centre: Chief OKW, Wehrmacht Adjutants, Admiral Voss, General Scherff must enter by Gate IIIA, vehicle by Gate IIA. Foot traffic to the Party Chancellery, to the personal Adjutants and the kitchens enter by Gate IA.

11. Couriers must not enter Security Zone A. Couriered material is to be delivered to an agreed place for immediate collection by the command centre in Security Zone A.

12. The entry gates to Security Zone A (Gate IA at Bunker 12, Gate IIA at the Reich Marshals house, Gate IIIA between Houses 7 and 77) are each manned by an Unteroffizier of the Führer-Grenade-Battalion and an RSD official. The duty of the Unteroffizier is to check the pass of all persons requiring entry. He may not allow any person to enter without a pass, except where the RSD sentry accompanies the visitor personally into Security Zone A. The passes of persons leaving the Security Zone are to be examined with the same attention to detail as those entering. In the event of any irregularity being detected, the visitor is to be brought to the guardhouse by the RSD sentry or the guard sent for.

13. Security Zone A will be constantly patrolled by one RSD official, who has the duty to monitor all persons and to escort unauthorized persons out of the Security Zone.

14. The same soldiers are always to be appointed as messengers for the Press and telex and issued with the appropriate pass.

15. By order of the Führer, the circle of persons dining in Dining Hall I of Officers Mess I is his closest entourage. Guests additional to this list and for meals at the Tea House will receive invitations from Obergruppenführer Schaub General Lieutenant Schmundt, or their respective deputies, only at the request of the Führer. Applications are to be submitted in good time.

16. All persons from outside who have been ordered into the presence of the Führer or to a command centre within Security Zone A must await their summons in Security Zone I and Dining Hall II, where they will be treated as guests of the Führer.

[Signed] Albert Bormann, NSKK-Gruppenführer
[Signed] Schmundt, General Lieutenant [24]

Those at the Wolf's Lair saw that the Hitler of late 1943 was unlike the confident Führer who had boarded his special train bound for the Polish front in September 1939. His dogged determination had not diminished, but his staff noticed that he had changed considerably since his time at his East Prussian headquarters and began to notice physical problems too. Sometimes his knees would begin to shake, or he had to quickly grab hold of his trembling left hand with his right. His left foot dragged upon the ground and he had slowly developed a prominent stoop. Everyone was astonished that he continued not to take his deteriorating symptoms very seriously. Morell took to giving him daily injections with various drugs, so that he would feel more comfortable, especially during the war conferences. Yet despite the effects of his health he was seen to be working as hard as ever and spending hours at a time in the damp, unhealthy climate of his bunker. Morell continually told his stubborn patient to leave the headquarters and spend time recuperating at his mountain retreat, but he ignored his doctor's pleas and preferred to stay on in East Prussia a sick man, spending a few days in bed at a time, but always appearing for the daily war conference.

By late 1943 he rarely came into contact with people outside the headquarters. The once sociable Führer had become a recluse. More and more he stayed in his bunker, restless and miserable. His only exercise and fresh air was had from an occasional stroll round the headquarters garden or woods, but even these became rarer and virtually non-existent when the snow showers arrived. Schaub and Schmundt tried their best to lift his spirits with new guests to the Wolf's Lair, and to enliven the evening parties with new conversation. But whatever they did, nothing could hide the fact that the war on the Eastern Front had become much worse. The last weeks of 1943 passed, like the autumn, in a sequence of bitter and bloodthirsty battles, which consequently sapped the will and energy of German forces almost beyond repair.

Christmas at the Wolf's Lair was dismal. Hitler almost completely ignored the festive season. There was no Christmas tree and not a single candle to celebrate. Despite many well-wishers sending greetings to the Führer in the East, this Christmas passed without the normal routine previously enjoyed by Hitler. Some of his closest staff found the mood depressing, and the atmosphere was filled with forced gaiety. There was light conversation among the guests, but they could not hide the fact that it was the worst Christmas they had spent at the Wolf's Lair.

Chapter V

Unshakeable Allegiance

The military situation on the Eastern Front in January 1944 was dire for the German Army. It had entered the New Year with a dwindling number of soldiers to man the battle lines. The Red Army, however, was in even greater strength than ever before and Hitler's reluctance to concede territory was still proving to be very problematic for the commanders in the field. The persistent lack of strategic direction in the East was causing major trouble too. In spite of the worsening conditions, the German Army were compelled to fight on.

At the Wolf's Lair, Hitler always began the New Year with optimism. He had convinced the German people to stand fast in the face of adversary and through their iron will and fortitude he promised them victory. In front of his war staff he radiated that same confidence and instilled them with fresh hope and strength of mind. But whatever assurances he gave them, January brought nothing but a string of familiar problems. By 15 January, news reached the Wolf's Lair that the Red Army had unleashed their much awaited winter offensive against Army Group North. Within days, reports confirmed that the Soviets had wrenched open the German front and poured powerful units through the decimated gaps. The 18th Army, which bore the brunt of the main attacks, were outnumbered by at least three divisions to one. As usual, the German troops were expected to hold the front, but the overwhelming enemy firepower proved too much and General Kuerchler's Army Group was forced to fall back under a hurricane of enemy fire. Within four days of the attack the Russians had successfully breached Army Group North's defences in three places. This effectively wrenched open a massive corridor allowing Red Army troops to pour through towards the besieged city of Leningrad. Troops of the 18th Army were beginning to disintegrate. Already there had been reports indicating that some 40,000 casualties had been incurred trying to contain the Soviets. Fighting in the mud and freezing water, the men were totally exhausted and unable to hold back the enemy for any appreciable length of time. Hitler was disgruntled by the collapse of the Front and sent a message to Kuerchler prohibiting all voluntary withdrawals and reserved all decisions to withdraw for himself.

In a drastic attempt to infuse determination in his generals and to strengthen faith in ultimate victory, Hitler decided to summon the principle generals from the Eastern Front to the Wolf's Lair on 26 January. Row upon row, they sat before him in the dining room of the converted inn at Security Zone II. After Morell had administered Hitler the usual injections, the Führer took to the stage and lectured them. He made it clear that all officers were to support the drive for ultimate victory and influence the conduct of operations by instilling in their men a fanatical resolve to fight in the name of National Socialism. He challenged his generals, telling them that that they must induct the seeds of National Socialism, and remain undiminished in their resolve to turn around the unfortunate circumstances that had befallen them on the Eastern Front. As Hitler paused in his speech, a deathly silence fell in the room. Suddenly, the silence was broken by a loud voice coming from the front row. Hitler glared; it was Manstein. There followed another silence, but this time it was icy, as if Hitler paused for effect, waiting for his generals to unanimously rise to their feet and applaud him. But there was neither, not even a murmur. On the rostrum, Hitler's face became contorted with anger. He scanned the room with indignation and stopped at Manstein and asked him harshly about his derisive behaviour. Hitler felt so insulted that his concentration broke and he felt unable to finish to the speech. Instead, he brought it to an abrupt end and stalked out of the room, unable to look at any of the generals. Within half an hour Manstein was ordered to report to the Führer's study. In a meeting that lasted only minutes, Hitler told Manstein that he would never tolerate such sarcastic behaviour again, and would not be interrupted either. Although at the evening conference Hitler's manner towards Manstein was cordial, he was never able to forgive the field-marshal for his behaviour that day.

During late January, Hitler decided to return to his mountain retreat. He joked that he wanted to be closer to the Italian front but remarked that he never dreamt he would one day need one so close to Italy. But the real reason that Hitler had decided to leave his East Prussian headquarters was his growing fear of an enemy air raid on the Wolf's Lair. In fact, he told Speer back in October 1943, that he had fully expected massive aerial daylight attacks on the headquarters, and for this reason he had ordered plans to be drawn up for the third construction period in order to strengthen the existing bunkers and to construct new ones. Caution too had also been taken to prevent the possibility of enemy troops being dropped into the compound, which was one of his greatest fears. Although it might have been difficult in the summer months on the few open spaces between the forests, swamps, lakes, due to the many thousands of mines surrounding large areas of the headquarters, he was becoming increasingly concerned that the enemy could be landed on frozen lakes. It was for this reason the Führer ordered anti-aircraft batteries to be installed that could fire point-blank at intruders, which could in effect smash the ice. In Goldap, some 50 miles north-east of the Wolf's Lair, a battalion of airborne troops were stationed and could be dropped into the headquarters at a moment's notice, should enemy troops have got in.

With the growing threat of attack on the headquarters, various degrees of alerts were introduced. There were four levels: 'alert readiness', 'alert', 'gas alert' and 'fire alert'. Alert readiness was communicated only by either telephone or runner, giving instructions to order the defence of the headquarters against a possible attack by aircraft, airborne landings, parachute troops, or saboteurs. If these alerts occured after dark, armbands were put on in order to distinguishthe enemy. Those without armbands after the sirens had sounded were to be regarded as the enemy and would be shot. All gas alerts were given by a gong, whilst blasts were given by telephone or by shouting *'gas!'*. Though the official procedure was, 'keep calm! Immediately put on gas-mask'. Other routine alert procedures were fire alerts, and these were signified over the telephone with calls or shouts of *'fire!'*

In order to tighten security, the two main telephone numbers of the Wolf's Lair were changed on 1 February, to prevent any unauthorized persons from obtaining telephone connections into the headquarters' telephone exchanges. This, however, had already happened. Weeks before, a great number of unauthorized persons managed to get connected to the HQ telephone exchanges by obtaining the numbers by telephone of the Rastenburg Post Office.

Although great efforts had been made to secure the headquarters from possible enemy attacks, and to increase security within the installation itself, problems still existed, especially with hundreds of labourers of Organization Todt brought in daily during the various construction stages. As the labourers poised to begin the last and final phase of construction, Hitler and staff left for Munich on 23 February. With Hitler's departure, hundreds of workers moved in to begin erecting even stronger bunkers to safeguard the Führer and the rest of the inhabitants of the Wolf's Lair from aerial attacks.

Now that supreme headquarters had moved to the Obersalzberg, Hitler continued presiding over important dilemmas of the War. The Eastern Front was still causing him much concern. Earlier in the month he had relieved General Kuechler for his failure to hold Army Group North together, and replaced him with General Walther Model. Model was regarded by the Führer as a great improviser who was capable of changing the tactical situation in Army Group North. Almost immediately Model went to work by introducing his '*Schild und Schwert*' (Shield and Sword) policy, which stated that no soldiers were to withdraw without express permission, and only if they paved the way for a counterstroke later. Model had assured Hitler that he was determined to prevent the front from degenerating into a panic flight and all stragglers would be collected and sent back to the line. He cancelled leaves, sent walking wounded to their units, and sent a number of the rear-echelon troops to the front. Without hesitation he requested more reinforcements, which included Waffen-SS replacements, naval coast batteries and Luftwaffe troops.

Throughout February Hitler was updated on Model's reforms, and by the time he had departed for Bavaria his faithful general had temporarily restored the frontline units. During March, however, the Red Army began exerting more pressure, especially against the 16th Army defending the Baltic. But the spring thaw had arrived early and melting snow had turned the roads on which the Russians were travelling into a quagmire. Model once again saw this as an opportunity and reinforced the front lines, bringing the Russian advance almost to a standstill. Thanks to Model, Army Group North was now stabilized. Due to his energetic, innovative and courageous method of leadership he had prevented the wholesale collapse of the northern sector of the Eastern Front.

Model's success in the north soon earned him a new command in Army Group South. On 30 March, less than a week before Army Group South was re-designated Army Group North Ukraine, Model replaced Manstein and was installed by Hitler as Commander-in-Chief.

For three long months Hitler and his war staff had watched Army Group South fight a series of bitter and bloody battles in order to stem the gradual deterioration of its forces in southern Russia. Conditions for the German Army between January and March were dismal. Supplies were inadequate, and replacements in men were far below what was needed to sustain its divisions along the entire front. To make matters worse, in January a 110-mile breach between Army Group Centre and Army Group South had developed. Both groups had sufficient forces to plug the gap, but by the end of the month the gap opened even wider when the Belorussian Front pushed the 2nd Army to the line of the Ipa River.

By early March, advanced Soviet units had reached the outskirts of the city of Tarnopol. Within days of their arrival Red Army troops advanced through the ravaged city but were soon beaten back by strong German defences. As German soldiers fought for Tarnopol, Hitler issued another order appealing for his forces on the Eastern Front to use towns, cities and surrounding areas as fortified positions in order to slow the Soviet drive westward. In total, Hitler designated some 26 cities and larger towns on still occupied Soviet territory as fortified positions.

In spite of the high casuality rate, the Wehrmacht and its Waffen-SS counterparts had generally defended their positions well against terrible odds. By early April the Red Army, after nearly eight months of continuous movement had at last given the Germans respite. Hitler once again felt that he alone had displayed nerves of steel in front of his demoralized generals. During the situation conferences, his commanders made a number of furtive attempts to abandon certain areas of land to the Russians. Hitler, however, had held strong, and prohibited any attempts by his commanders to make deep withdrawals.

Whilst the Eastern Front offered nothing but a string of catastrophes, there was now growing uncertainty about the Anglo-American invasion of northern France. At Klessheim castle, a few miles away from the Berghof, Hitler once again took to the stage and repeated the view that the enemy would invade in Normandy and Brittany, and not the much closer Channel coast in the Pas de Calais area. On 1 May, Hitler impatiently wanted information relating to the prospects of Marck's Corps being able to defend Normandy. At the war conference the next day Hitler boldly announced he was to insert stronger forces into the Normandy and Brittany peninsulas, including a paratrooper corps.

By early June Hitler received reports that German counter-intelligence had begun monitoring increased radio traffic from the BBC. From these decoded messages it was fairly certain that the invasion would start within the next fourteen days. What was also revealing about the messages was the fact that they were addressed to resistance groups located in the area of Lille/Amiens, Normandy and Brittany.

By the time Hitler was awakened at 9.00 am on 6 June, wave after wave of enemy landing craft had disgorged tanks and men onto the landing beaches of Normandy. Over the days that followed, further intelligence reports of the Allied invasion continued to elude Hitler and his war staff.

OKH still believed, and so did Rommel, that the attack on Normandy was not the main assault, which would come somewhere in the Pas de Calais area. Throughout June and early July this view held sway at the supreme headquarters and influenced decisions. The formidable 15th Army was held back and did not come to the aid of the 7th Army, which was already involved in heavy fighting in the Normandy sector. Within two weeks, reports confirmed that the Normandy landings had been successful, the high casualty rate notwithstanding.

Whilst the Western Front offered no real comfort, events in the East were far grimmer. By the middle of June Hitler was already torn between remaining at the Berghof and directing the War in the West, or returning to his Wolf's Lair and overseeing operations in the East. The third anniversary of the invasion of the Soviet Union was marked with a foreboding that not even Hitler himself could have ever imagined. During the early hours of 22 June, across vast parts of Army Group Centre the front line erupted in a wall of flame and smoke. Almost 22,000 guns and mortars and 2,000 Katyusha multiple rocket launchers poured fire and destruction on to German defensive positions. By the end of the first day of the Russian attack the situation for Army Group Centre looked grim. All along the front, battered and blasted German units had tried in vain to hold their positions using First World War tactics against overwhelming odds.

For the Soviets, their summer offensive had progressed well and the city of Vitebsk was almost surrounded. At the situation conference held on 25 June, it was reported that the Red Army were slowly and systematically bulldozing their way through with German forces either fighting to the death, or saving themselves by escaping the impending slaughter by withdrawing to another makeshift position. According to an army officer's report, the ferocity of the Soviet attacks was immense and without respite. After four long days of almost continuous fighting, German troops were exhausted and battling for survival in a number of places. Hitler insisted that his troops must fight from fixed positions without any tactical retreat, but according to Keitel this had caused many units to become encircled by Red Army rifle divisions, leaving tank units to speed past unhindered and achieve deeper penetrations.

By 26 June, the Red Army had achieved a number of successful encirclements. Around the city of Bobruysk for instance, a total of 70,000 troops belonging to the 9th Army were trapped in the city and to the east of it. Once again OKH instructed that every soldier must hold every foot of ground, forbidding any type of withdrawal. As a result of this stubborn order, Soviet divisions closed in around the city of Bobruysk. The situation for the

9th Army was critical, and the area around the shattered city had become a vast killing ground. In just two days of fighting it was reported that some 10,000 German troops had been killed around the city, with another 6,000 captured.

During the last days of June, the Soviet summer offensive took much of Hitler's attention, far more than operations unfolding in the West. Here in the killing fields of the Soviet Union he was aware that the outcome of the attack that fateful summer would be more catastrophic than that experienced by his brave legions on the Western Front. By 28 June the situation for Army Group Centre was dismal. General Zeitzler reported to Hitler that General Busch had cabled him, telling him that his 9th Army had been significantly damaged with high losses. The 4th Army was retreating, and the 3rd Panzer Army was in a critical state, with one corps left out of its original three.

Hitler demanded that all three armies stop withdrawing immediately and hold a new line due north, south of Beresino. Busch wasted no time and instructed the three armies to halt, but the damage inflicted on them was far beyond repair. Hitler was incensed over what he saw as Busch's dilatory tactics and finally decided to replace him with Field Marshal Model, hoping to instil new vigour and restore determination into Army Group Centre. The change of command pleased many commanders in the field. Many of them had been bitter over developments, which they felt resulted from the way that Army Group Centre had been led. Hitler knew that out on the battlefield his 'troubleshooter' would try his utmost to minimize the extent of the disaster. With 28 of its 37 divisions already destroyed or surrounded, Model was called upon by his Führer to rescue the remnants and stabilize the front to avoid complete annihilation.

Whilst Model gave his best to bring about stability in Army Group Centre, on 9 July Hitler decided to fly back to the Wolf's Lair for one day. When he arrived the headquarters was in turmoil; hundreds of Todt labourers were still busily working in shifts turning the previous bunkers of Security Zone I into gigantic concrete forts. But Hitler had not come back to oversee construction, he had flown there specifically on a mission to instil confidence in his weary commanders. Early that afternoon he gathered his Eastern commanders for a conference and spoke at length about the looming threat to the frontiers of the Reich, and his deep concerns about the possibility that East Prussia might even be invaded. The defence of East Prussia, he warned, would be the last battle in the East. He told his commanders that they must remain optimistic if they were to succeed. Although many left the conference that afternoon imbued with new courage and fortitude, they could still not miss the underlying atmosphere at the headquarters, which indicated that the War had taken a very bad turn for the worse.

Even as Hitler flew back to the Berghof later that day, high drama gripped the Wolf's Lair as further reports were received on Army Group Centre. With nothing but a string of defeats and unable to improve the terrible situation, Model finally informed OKH that Army Group Centre could no longer assemble a projected attack north of Vilnius in time to halt the Russian armour – Army Group North would have to do it and suffer the consequences.

By 13 July the Russian summer offensive had fulfilled its objectives and left Army Group Centre almost totally destroyed. The rapid Soviet advance had taken the Army Group by complete surprise and had consequently bypassed a number of large German troop concentrations on the frontline in the 3rd Panzer Army and 9th Army sectors. Although remnants of these forces managed to claw their way west to the relative safety of Army Group North, its once proud forces were a mere shadow of their former selves. The badly beaten and bruised divisions had arrived east of Lithuania and to the east of the frontier of Poland with most of their units crushed.

In total, OKH estimated that between 25 and 30 divisions were badly mauled during the three weeks of constant fighting, with 17 divisions totally annihilated. Losses in troops were hard to gauge, but it was believed that some 300,000 were killed and captured.

The plan to 'pull the teeth' of the Red Army for the rest of the summer so that it could not undertake offensive operations and to shorten the front by eliminating the Soviet 'bulge' around Kursk had been an utter failure. Hitler was well aware of the implications. Even the Normandy landings were not such a huge disaster. The great westward retreat that would begin in September, giving up almost all territory east of the Dnieper, was the direct result of the failure of Citadel.

On 15 July, Hitler returned once more to the Wolf's Lair, but this time to stay and direct the war on the Eastern Front more closely. When he arrived, the installation still resembled a building site. Security Zone I was almost unrecognizable. In place of small, low bunkers were huge concrete and iron structures looming skyward, their roofs expertly camouflaged by transplanted grass and trees. Many buildings were reinforced, and new, elaborate ones constructed using thousands of cubic metres of concrete. Göring, for instance, had an enormous bunker built east of his house overlooking the main railway line. Running west, just north of the Bormann bunker, a huge general purpose bunker had also been built. On the main Security Zone I road, west of the Keitel bunker, were low bunker/barracks-type buildings for the Führer's personnel and SS adjutants (No. 8), and another (No. 13) for his *Wehrmacht* adjutant, Schmundt, who was also chief of the Army Personnel Office. The building was still scaffolded, being enlarged and joined together and shaped like a large 'M'. West (No. 8) bunker, there was a bunker/barracks building, L-shaped, for various liaison personnel posted to the headquarters.

Owing to the extensive reconstruction of the area and the finishing touches to the *Führerbunker*, yet another inner security zone was established, known as the Führer Security Zone. This was located in the north-west corner of Security Zone I. Its fence encircled the guest bunker (No. 15) where Hitler was to live during this period and a barracks-type building taken over as the situation barracks, or *Lagebaracke* or *Lagehaus*, until the *Führerbunker* was completed. Hitler was to sleep in a small, cramped room in the eastern end of the south wing of the guest bunker.

There was also an area enclosed by a fence erected south-west of Security Zone I. Most of the key sections of the army's operations staff were located in this sector and continued to be responsible for working the Führer conference pronouncements into meaningful form for issue to the staffs at OKH, OKL and OKW. The old *Kurhaus* became a casino for the headquarters personnel who lived and worked in the area. A huge telephone exchange too had been built in the southern part of this sector.

To the east, south of Security Zone I, there were now buildings for guests and Ribbentrop's liaison staff. A little further east, on a road in Security Zone II, two massive, abutting general purpose bunkers (No. 54) were still being constructed as shelters for that area of the Wolf's Lair.

In this final construction period that continued until January 1945, many of the old bunkers, including Hitler's own bunker and wooden annex, received additional shells of at least 4 metres of steel and concrete, making them completely windowless. The *Führerbunker* was to depend entirely on artificial air supply when the several doors and air intakes, which were fitted with gas protection chambers, were closed. The shell ceiling of the bunker alone was 5 metres thick, giving a total thickness of the two ceilings of at least 7 metres. This was considered more than enough protection against the heaviest possible aerial attacks. The immediate layer of gravel was designed to cushion and prevent damage to the inner bunker. Although enemy aircraft were frequently seen flying over the headquarters, it was suggested that there was no real immediate danger to the Führer's safety. But Hitler still felt he could leave absolutely nothing to chance. He was constantly aware of the advancing Red Army and increasingly concerned that a special unit might be assigned to attack the Wolf's Lair, either by parachuting into the installation or mounting a ground assault. In order to strengthen the protection of the headquarters he had ordered that a massive minefield belt containing some 54,000 mines be laid inside the outer perimeter, within Security Zone III. Here the minefields were boarded by a double-apron barbed wire chain link fence with warning signs. The area was regarded so dangerous that eleven members of Hitler's entourage, including the secretaries, who had a tendency to wander around the barrier, signed a document outlining that they had been fully informed about the minefield's existence.

Over a period of months the headquarters was transformed into a huge fortress of concrete and wood. The noon conferences were temporarily moved to one of these hutments in the situation barrack of the Führer's Restricted Zone. Two partition walls had been knocked down to create the long makeshift conference room, allowing more light and air to pass through the open windows, and to fill the hut with the smell of the surrounding woods.

The heat during July was oppressive. Hitler spent most of his time working in the new bunkers, which were much cooler than the stuffy wooden barracks. But his poor health, coupled with the hot weather was bothering him. The adjutants did their best to keep their Führer in the best of spirits, but it normally did not last long. It had become quite noticeable to Hitler's staff that the heat was causing him to become more irritable and irrational. One such episode of his irrational behaviour was during a conference on 18 July. Whilst he was conferring with his war staff, pouring over maps, he became very annoyed that a winged insect was interrupting his concentration. He suddenly turned to one of his SS adjutants and accused him of disrupting the conference by not using his initiative and removing the insect. Later that day his staff was shocked to hear that he had dismissed the young adjutant and had him transferred to the Eastern Front. Such unreasonable behaviour staggered his intimate circle. Lunching with Fraulein Schroder however, she noticed how relaxed Hitler seemed, but he stunned her by mentioning that he had premonitions of something terrible was going to happen to him.

On 20 July, Hitler rose earlier than normal as Mussolini was expected after lunch. The regular 1 pm war conference was brought forward 30 minutes and Keitel was advised he must make it as brief as possible as Hitler was meeting the Duce. At about 12.25 pm, Hitler walked the 40 yards or so to the usual grey camouflaged conference hut, finding Warlimont and twenty other staff officers waiting outside. Although it was cloudy and rain was in the air the weather was warm and stuffy and as a consequence all the windows to the hut were open. Guarding the hut was an SS guard and an RSD patrol in the area. Inside, there was a sergeant operating a small telephone switchboard, and in the conference room two SS officers. One of them, Gunsche, and the other Himmler's liaison man *SS-Gruppenführer* Herman Fegelein greeted Hitler and the twenty officers as they gathered around the long, narrow, oak map table. Only Hitler used a chair, his back to the door, at the middle of the table. A pair of spectacles rested on the map. Playing with a magnifying glass in one hand, which he now needed at the conferences to read the print on the maps, he began listening to General Heusinger, who was standing to his right, briefing him on the Eastern Front. Shortly afterwards, Keitel broke in to announce the presence of General Fromm's chief of staff, a one-armed, one-eyed colonel holding a yellow briefcase. Hitler and a few other staff officers had recognized this colonel from a meeting with them five days earlier. Keitel announced to Hitler that this was Colonel Count Schenk von Stauffenberg who was to brief him on the new divisions. With composure, the Colonel raised his left hand in a Hitler salute. Hitler then shook Stauffenberg's mutilated hand, and sat down again, announcing that before he heard his report he was to finish listening to Heusinger first.

Whilst the General busily reported on the situation at the front, Hitler leaned over the map table, using his elbow as support. Using various coloured pencils in his left hand he made alterations to the map whilst Heusinger continued to talk. As he began to conclude his report by telling them about withdrawing forces from Lake Peipus there was suddenly a tremendous, blinding flash. Heusinger's explanation came to an abrupt end as the room exploded. Outside officers and guards dived for cover as an avalanche of debris from the hut blew out through the windows and roof. A number of passing officers also took cover behind trees and parked vehicles, fearing that the headquarters was under direct aerial attack.

Inside the hut, thick smoke filled the room. A number of staff officers were buried beneath the debris. Admiral Puttkamer was in a state of shock, and through the dust and pieces of building he noticed a twisted heater under the window and thought it had exploded, but then realized it was the summer. He then immediately thought that foreign labourers who were working on the new bunkers had attacked the hut. Many others caught in the explosion thought that the headquarters was under attack, and feared leaving the hut, thinking that they might suddenly blunder straight into enemy fire. The majority though were in complete shock and those that could stand hurriedly clambered across the wreckage through the charred fragments of maps and papers, out to the fresh air, coughing and spluttering. Keitel had been blown on his back by the explosion and for a moment he could hear nothing except sounds of groaning men in pain. He slowly pulled himself up and struggled towards a figure lying near the left door jamb – it was the Führer. Hitler had been stunned by the explosion, but also feared leaving the building, worried that there had been a paratroop attack on the installation. Painfully he stumbled to his feet, beating out the flames on his shredded black trousers. Supported by Keitel and Sonnleiter, who had assured the Führer that that the headquarters was not under enemy attack, they shuffled into the corridor and then out the door.

Inside the security zone all was a hive of confused activity as first aid personnel, guards and officers waving their pistols were seen running to and fro. Whilst being supported by Keitel, Hitler momentarily paused for composure, relieved to have survived the explosion, and then looked back at the smouldering hut. Keitel exclaimed that it must have been one of the Todt workmen but Hitler immediately rebuked his General and declared confidently that no workman would ever lift a hand against him. As Hitler unsteadily limped past all the confusion, one of his adjutants called for Hasselbach and Morell. Inside the bunker Hitler took a seat to relieve the discomfort and took his own pulse. His three secretaries immediately arrived and to their surprise saw their Führer grinning at them with a smoke-blackened face. Traudl Junge almost burst into laughter at the sight of his hair, which resembled a scarecrow's. Afterwards he retired into his bedroom to let Hasselbach and Morell remove his tattered trousers. Both doctors noticed that he had been wounded on both thighs by the explosion and had to carefully remove over 100 fragmented splinters from his legs. His face was also cut in many places, and his forehead had received a deep cut from a falling roof timber. Though Hitler appeared outwardly composed despite the whole trauma, inside he was a man steeled for revenge. Without resting he immediately sent out guards to search for additional bombs hidden inside the headquarters and ordered the injured and deafened Colonel von Below to the telephone exchange to forbid the telephonists from using the switchboard. All security guards at the gates into the Wolf's Lair were ordered not to allow any persons out under any pretext, and those entering the installation were first frisked for hidden weapons, and accompanied to their place of business. The outer gate was immediately closed, obstacles were placed in the roadway, and the guards were ordered not to allow any persons through.

Apparently, new pass procedures inside the Führer's Restricted Zone had not been set up in the short time since the headquarters had been moved back from the Berghof. Although there were only a very small number of people allowed to enter, and only on legitimate business, both the SS and RSD guards who had been patrolling the Führer's Restricted Zone were shocked by the lack of security that they themselves had imposed. To increase Hitler's safety, during the night of 20/21 July elements of Hitler's personal bodyguard detachment, the *Leibstandarte-SS Adolf Hitler*, arrived and occupied all major points inside the compound, sealing off Security Zone I. In the course of just 24 hours SS guards were added to every FBB post inside and outside the headquarters. In addition, an entire SS alert unit was employed inside Security Zone I, much to the resentment of the regular headquarter troops.

Despite the increased security measures, Hitler refused to rest, and at about 1.15 pm, he emerged from his bunker, wearing a new uniform. To the surprise of his staff he insisted on wandering by himself, deliberately making a point of chatting with the construction workers to let them know they were not under any suspicion. Strolling in sight of the Führer Zone's perimeter fence, Hitler was clearly totally unhurt by the explosion. Watching from a distance, his adjutant guessed that he wanted to show everyone at the Wolf's Lair that he was very much alive.

Fraulein Schroder wrote in her diary:

I did not expect to be called in for lunch with him [Hitler] after the assassination attempt. But nevertheless I was sent for to join him. I was astounded to see how fresh he looked, and how sprightly he stepped toward me. He described to me how his servants had reacted to the news: [Heinz] Linge was indignant, Arndt had begun to cry. Then he said, verbatim, 'Believe me, this is the turning point for Germany. From now on things will look up again. I'm glad the schweinehunde have unmasked themselves!'[25]

Over lunch with Fraulein Schroder, Hitler reported what had happened in detail and proudly exhibited his tattered and burnt black trousers. He was sure, he said, that his miraculous escape from death was a clear indication that he was guided by the hand of God. He openly admitted that the War was in a perilous situation, but he confidently asserted that surviving the assassination attempt was evidence that the War would turn in Germany's favour. With fresh new courage and optimism he said that he was looking forward to the Duce's visit.

After the meal he was driven to the small railway platform adjoining the Wolf's Lair where he met his old ally. As Mussolini stepped onto the platform at 2.30 pm, Hitler warmly embraced him and immediately revealed what had happened earlier that day. Security was tighter than ever before and on their return to Security Zone I an assortment of armoured vehicles could be seen accompanied by well armed Waffen-SS soldiers. Yet, in spite of the increased security that day, the source of the explosion was still unknown. Hitler did learn that the bomb had blown a deep hole into the conference hut floor, which evidently pointed to a bomb being planted with a timing device of some kind. He was aware that only a handful of officers had known that the war conference would be brought forward because of the Duce's visit. It was some hours later when hard evidence revealed what had actually happened. A sergeant who had operated the telephone switchboard outside the conference room reported to Bormann that a one-eyed colonel, who had informed him he was expecting a long-distance call from Berlin, had come out of the conference room and without even waiting, hurriedly departed without even his cap, belt and his recognizable yellow briefcase. He was seen walking over to building 8/13, where his aide and General Fellgiebel were standing, and waited. When the great explosion was heard, passing officers watched as the general and his aide climbed into a staff car, which passed the situation hut, and sped off making its way to the Führer's security gate. According to an RSHA report the General was Stauffenberg. He and his aide bluffed their way through two checkpoints. At Security Zone I checkpoint Stauffenberg had said to the FBB and RSD guards that he had an urgent order of the Führer's and even having heard the explosions they still allowed them through. Stauffenberg went into the southern guard house and telephoned to one of the headquarters commandant's officers, Captain von Leonhard Mollendorf, whom he knew very well and had had breakfast with that morning. Mollendorf immediately ordered the guard to let Stauffenberg and Haeften pass. They then proceeded to the airfield and left East Prussian soil forever.

Hitler insisted on taking his old Italian collaborator to the smoking debris of the conference hut, and gave him a guided tour, reliving the moment Stauffenburg nearly took his life. Although Hitler had emerged with minimal injuries, his staff caught the brunt of the explosion. Those who had been on his right had suffered worst. General Korton had been impaled by a table leg, Schmundt had terrible leg injuries and lost an eye, Stenographer Berger had lost both legs and died of his horrific injuries later that day, Colonel Heinz Brandt lost a foot.* Mussolini was horrified and amazed that such a thing could have happened at the Wolf's Lair.

---

* Colonel Heinz Brandt was chief of operations division of the general staff. He had also been an accomplice in the assassination attempt, but had not been warned to leave the conference hut before the explosion.

1 The ruined building of the Security Service and SS barracks. *HITM, courtesy of the Wolfschanze Museum in Ketrzyn*

2 The Detective Security Detail building. *HITM, courtesy of the Wolfschanze Museum in Ketrzyn*

3 Building that housed the SS-Escort Detachment and Hitler's personal servants. *HITM, courtesy of the Wolfschanze Museum in Ketrzyn*

4 The guest bunker in Security Zone I. *HITM, courtesy of the Wolfschanze Museum in Ketrzyn*

5 The guest bunker in Security Zone I. *HITM, courtesy of the Wolfschanze Museum in Ketrzyn*

6 The guest bunker flak tower. *HITM, courtesy of the Wolfschanze Museum in Ketrzyn*

7 The *Führerbunker* from the north east. *HITM, courtesy of the Wolfschanze Museum in Ketrzyn*

8 The *Führerbunker. HITM, courtesy of the Wolfschanze Museum in Ketrzyn*

9 A group of Wehrmacht soldiers rest during the early phase of *Barbarossa* in June 1941. The German attack took the Red Army by complete surprise. *HITM*

10 Hitler's bunker (No.11), known as the *Führerbunker*, was the main structure in Security Zone I within the Wolf's Lair, the location of the fateful decisions concerning Operation *Barbarossa*. *HITM, courtesy of the Wolfschanze Museum in Ketrzyn*

11 A doorway at the side of the *Führerbunker. HITM, courtesy of the Wolfschanze Museum in Ketrzyn*

12 The *Führerbunker. HITM, courtesy of the Wolfschanze Museum in Ketrzyn*

13 The ruined building of Hitler's adjutants army personnel office. *HITM, courtesy of the Wolfschanze Museum in Ketrzyn*

14 The building that once housed Hitler's SS-Escort detachment. It is now a restaurant and hotel. *HITM, courtesy of the Wolfschanze Museum in Ketrzyn*

15 *Göringbunker. HITM, courtesy of the Wolfschanze Museum in Ketrzyn*

16 Entrance to the *Göringbunker. HITM, courtesy of the Wolfschanze Museum in Ketrzyn*

17 Göringbunker. Part of the railway line is visible in this image. *HITM, courtesy of the Wolfschanze Museum in Ketrzyn*

18 Steel steps that led to the roof of the bunker which housed flak guns. *HITM, courtesy of the Wolfschanze Museum in Ketrzyn*

19 Wehrmacht soldiers move forward into action during the opening stages of *Barbarossa*. Both OKW and OKH looked upon these first exhilarating days of the campaign as confirming an aura of invincibility comparable to that of Napoleon's *Grande Armée*, which would prove an apt parallel. *HITM*

20 The remains of Göring's house that was constructed near the *Göringbunker* along the railway line. *HITM, courtesy of the Wolfschanze Museum in Ketrzyn*

28 Adjacent to Hitler's office. *Courtesy of Roger Bender/National Archives*

29 Hitler's dining room (Kasino I). *Courtesy of Roger Bender/National Archives*

30 Registration table. *Courtesy of Roger Bender/National Archives*

31 Hitler at the window of his private coach on board his *Führersonderzug* in 1941. *HITM*

32 Telephone Exchange building. *Courtesy of Roger Bender/National Archives*

33 Teletype office. *Courtesy of Roger Bender/National Archives*

34 Telex room. *Courtesy of Roger Bender/National Archives*

35 Hitler attends an SS dinner in his honour. During the War Hitler relied heavily on his foremost fighting machine to spearhead attacks, but by the later stages was compelled to use them more and more in defensive roles to try to hold back the Russian advance. *HITM*

36 A typical office at the Wolf's Lair. Many of these buildings were decorated in light panelled wood. *Courtesy of Roger Bender/National Archives*

37 Hitler's 'Desert Fox' confers with one of his staff officers during operations in the desert in North Africa. By late 1942 Hitler felt that Rommel had become pessimistic and had lost his nerve. *HITM*

38 The main kitchens at the Wolf's Lair. *Courtesy of Roger Bender/National Archives*

39 The mailroom. *Courtesy of Roger Bender/National Archives*

40 Hitler is pictured here with Mussolini and Göring during one of the Duce's visits to the Wolf's Lair. *HITM*

41 Göring holding his Field Marshal's baton during a conference held outside at the Wolf's Lair with some of his Luftwaffe commanders. *HITM*

42 Soldiers of 'Das Reich' during the initial stages of 'Citadel' in early July 1943. The German attack on the Kursk salient was a bold move, which Hitler hoped would bring him thousands of prisoners and stall the Russian onslaught westward for the summer. *HITM, Michael Cremin*

43 A very famous photograph taken at the Wolf's Lair on 15 July 1944. From left to right: General Klaus von Stauffenberg, Admiral Karl-Jesko von Puttkamer, General Karl Bodenschatz (back to camera), Hitler and General Wilhelm Keitel meet between the situation conference barrack and the Guest bunker. *National Archives*

44 Hitler's private office. *National Archives*

45 Weary Waffen-SS troops in a frozen trench in the winter of 1944. Hitler was determined that the Baltic States of Estonia, Latvia and Lithuania would be held. In his eyes these three countries were the last bastion of defence before the Reich. *HITM*

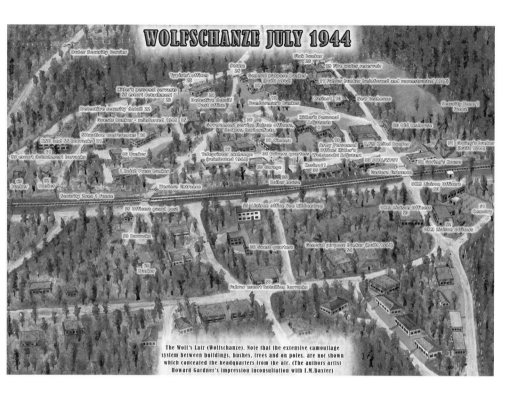

WOLFSCHANZE JULY 1944

Outer Security Barrier

Flak bunker
28

29 Fire water reservoir

Sauna
26

Typists' offices
25

General purpose bunker
(built 1944)
27

11 Fuhrer bunker (reinforced and reconstructed 1944)

Hitler's personal servants
55 escort detachment
23

Detective detail
24

Post office
Bombermen's bunker
12

Kasino1 14

New teahouse

Security Zone 1
Fence

Detective security detail 21

Hitler's Personal
Adjutants

Guests bunker - reinforced 1944 15

Government service liaison officers,
doctors, barbers, etc.

10 Old teahouse

Situation conferences 20

19 Cinema

Army Personnel
15 Official Hitler's
Wehrmacht Adjutant

16
2, FM Keitel bunker

11 Goring's bunker
(built 1944)

RSD and SS barracks 31

Teleprinter exchange
(reinforced 1944)

18 Drivers quarters

38 JODL/WFST

22 Goring's House

55 escort detachment barracks

40 Bunker

1 Reich Press bunker

19 Garage

Kasino11

Eastern Entrance

63
Bunker

62
Bunker

35
Boiler House

OKM Liaison Officers
50

Security Zone 1 Fence

Western Entrance

58 Officers guard post

55 Liaison office Von Ribbentrop

OKM Liaison Officers
53

51
Cemetery

52
OKM Liaison Officers

59 Barracks

56 Guest quarters

General purpose bunker (built 1944)
54

60
Bunker

57
Fuhrer escort batallion barracks

The Wolf's Lair (Wolfschanze). Note that the extensive camouflage
system between buildings, bushes, trees and on poles, are not shown
which concealed the headquarters from the air. (The authors artist
Howard Gardner's impression inconsultation with I.M.Baxter)

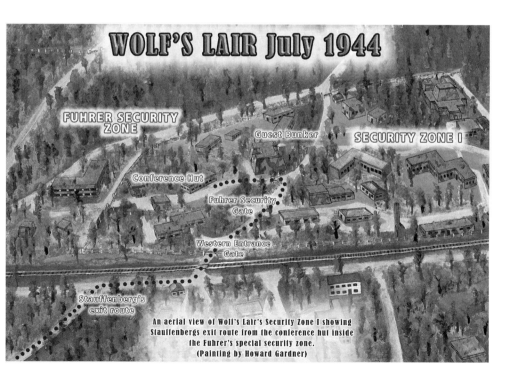

WOLF'S LAIR July 1944

FUHRER SECURITY
ZONE

Guest Bunker

SECURITY ZONE I

Conference Hut

Fuhrer Security
Gate

Western Entrance
Gate

Stauffenberg's
exit route

An aerial view of Wolf's Lair's Security Zone I showing
Stauffenbergs exit route from the conference hut inside
the Fuhrer's special security zone.
(Painting by Howard Gardner)

'Wolfschanze'

 Re-inforced concrete and steel   Gravel

"Wolfschanze" HQ, diagram of reinforced bunker

These additional shells were constructed with at least 4 metres of steel and concrete. The intermediate layer of gravel was poured in to provide cushioning against enemy bombs up to 10,000 kilograms.

48 Old bunker. *Reproduced from the author's private collection*

WOLFSCHANZE

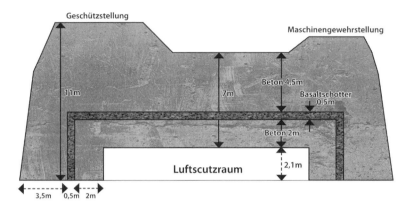

Luftschutzbunker von H. Göring (Längsschnitt).

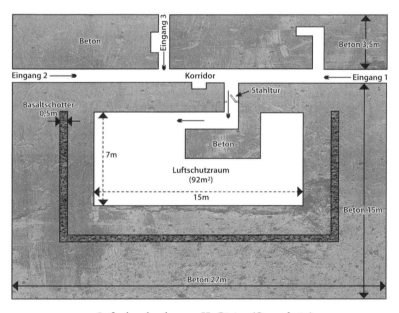

Luftschutzbunker von H. Göring (Querschnitt).

49 Göringbunker. Reproduced from the author's private collection

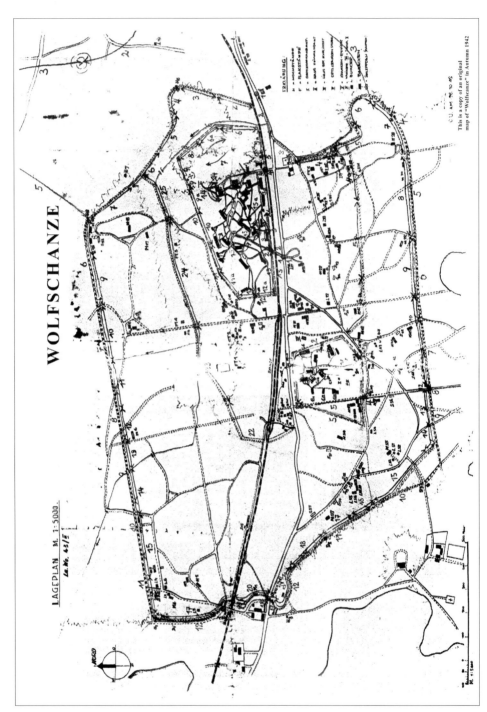

50 Wolfschanze Map, 1942.

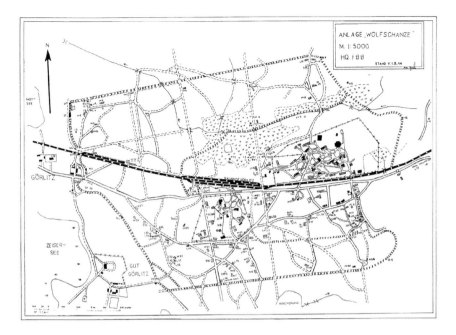

51 Wolfschanze Map, 1944.

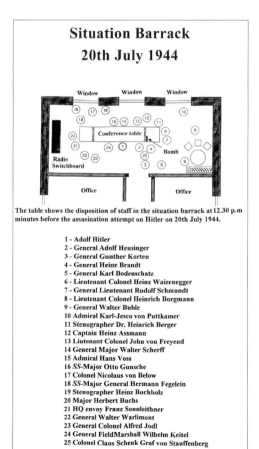

Situation Barrack
20th July 1944

Window   Window   Window

Conference table

Bomb

Radio
Switchboard

Office   Office

The table shows the disposition of staff in the situation barrack at 12.30 p.m
minutes before the assasination attempt on Hitler on 20th July 1944.

1 - Adolf Hitler
2 - General Adolf Heusinger
3 - General Gunther Korten
4 - General Heinz Brandt
5 - General Karl Bodenschatz
6 - Lieutenant Colonel Heinz Waizenegger
7 - General Lieutenant Rudolf Schmundt
8 - Lieutenant Colonel Heinrich Borgmann
9 - General Walter Buhle
10 Admiral Karl-Jesco von Puttkamer
11 Stenographer Dr. Heinrich Berger
12 Captain Heinz Assmann
13 Liutenant Colonel John von Freyend
14 General Major Walter Scherff
15 Admiral Hans Voss
16 *SS*-Major Otto Gunsche
17 Colonel Nicolaus von Below
18 *SS*-Major General Hermann Fegelein
19 Stenographer Heinz Buchholz
20 Major Herbert Buchs
21 HQ envoy Franz Sonnleithner
22 General Walter Warlimont
23 General Colonel Alfred Jodl
24 General FieldMarshall Wilhelm Keitel
25 Colonel Claus Schenk Graf von Stauffenberg

52 Diagram of the assassination
attempt, 20 July 1944.

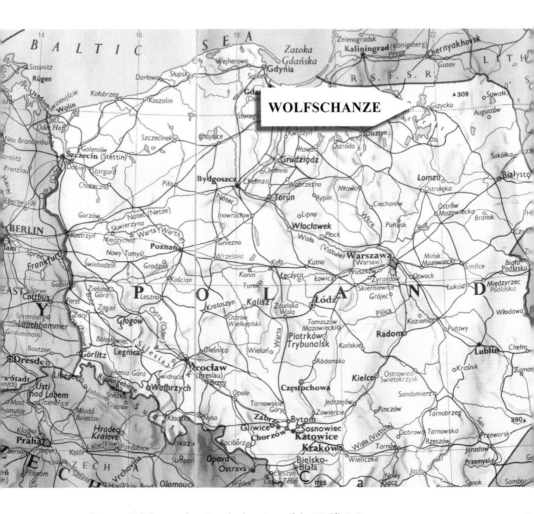

53 Postwar Polish map showing the location of the Wolf's Lair.

Afterwards, in the rain they walked out of the wreckage down the path to resume discussion at five o'clock in the headquarters mess. On the way Hitler walked over to the wire fence and was once more seen speaking with the Todt workers. He told them that they did not need to fear anything and that his investigators (RSHA) had found the real criminal. At tea he spoke at length with the Duce, but was constantly being interrupted by telephone calls from generals who wanted to know if the report of his death was true. After the tea party, which continued until about 7.00 pm, Mussolini bade Hitler a warm goodbye. After putting on his coat, the Duce was ushered into the light drizzle, never to see the Führer again.

By this time, encouraging reports from Berlin reached the headquarters that an attempted military revolt by a number of prominent officers, including Stauffenburg, had been stopped. All that was now needed to bring about an end to the conspiracy was to prove that Hitler was not dead. This was done over the telephone that evening by Hitler to Major Otto Remer, commander of the Berlin troops guarding the government building.

With the military revolt shut down the hours of anxiety and mystery at the Wolf's Lair were finally over. The atmosphere at the headquarters was now like one never experienced before. Hitler was determined that never again would anyone raise a hand against him or his leadership. What came next were loud protestations of loyalty from the General Staff. Almost immediately, to assure the Führer of their solemn devotion, Keitel ordered Warlimont to inform the commanders in chief in all OKW theatres of war of the attempted military coup by telephone. At the same time OKH was to tell commanders on the Eastern Front what had happened at the headquarters. In order to pledge his undying allegiance to the Führer publicly, Jodl personally decided to make a fanatical speech over at Security Zone II to the officers of the staff. Meanwhile, Bormann decided to inform the Gauleiters, using his modern teleprinter linkup.

At the 10 pm war conference Hitler began by expressing the sad loss to the two stenographers over the death of their colleague, Berger. The conference continued with discussions relating to operations on the Western Front and then dealing with the climactic showdown in the East.

During the second half of July the German position in Russia was as bad as ever. Army Group North Ukraine had tried its best to hold positions on the River Bug, whilst remnants of the battered and worn Army Group Centre were attempting to create a solid front on the line Kaunas, Bialystok-Brest and assemble forces on both its flanks. Plans were put forward at the conference to strike north and south to restore contact with both neighbouring groups. Army Group Centre was far too weak to reverse the deteriorating situation and the Russians had already begun rolling through its shattered front, bearing down toward the River Vistula. During this period, alarming reports confirmed that Soviet forces would soon be within striking distance of the Vistula. This meant that the Soviets would then be able to secure a bridgehead in the suburbs of Warsaw itself. In spite of the terrible situation left by the destruction of the centre of the front, by incredible application of military skill and courage, coupled with the fact that the Red Army's offensive was showing signs of slowing down, it was predicted that the line of the central sector of the front would be temporarily stabilized. In no more than six weeks the Russians had bulldozed their way westward covering more than 450 miles, but were finally slowing down east of Warsaw, having for the time being outstripped their supplies.

While news confirmed that the Eastern Front was beginning to show signs of stabilizing, Hitler terminated the conference. Afterwards, he wandered over to the tea house where he had assembled his entire staff to hear him read a hastily drafted message to the nation. The secretaries, adjutants, Keitel with bandaged hands, Jodl with a white bandage around his head, and others too who were wearing cuts and grazes on their faces and hands, all stood quietly to hear their Führer's recorded speech to the nation. It was broadcast at 1 pm.

Soon after his impassioned speech, which he hoped would bring the nation together in steadfastness, he retired to his bunker where he was again checked by Dr Morell. He was given an analgesic and a tranquilizer before going to sleep. His inner circle waited in the tea house until Morell returned to announce that the Führer's health was satisfactory. Yet, despite Morell's encouraging words, the assassination attempt had affected Hitler's health more than many people realized. He could hear nothing with his right ear and his eyes constantly flickered to the right. In fact, while taking one of his strolls around the headquarters that evening, he twice wandered off the path.

The next day, despite a persistent pain in his ear and appeals from his doctors to rest, he insisted on visiting his wounded officers at the nearby field hospital. On his arrival he found to his sorrow that two were on the edge of death. Schmundt was in a very bad way indeed. Trying to compose himself, Hitler spoke to Assmann and Puttkamer, who shared a room. Sitting on the end of Assmann's bed, he expressed his sorrow for what had happened and spoke about the vile treachery that lurked in the General Staff.

Later that day, the pain in Hitler's ear became much worse and caused him so much discomfort that Morell summoned Dr Erwin Giesing from the field hospital, the ear, nose and throat specialist. After examining his patient, Geising found that the eardrum was badly ruptured, the inner ear was damaged and that there appeared to be infection. Although Hitler was now convinced that he would never hear with his right ear again, he remained optimistic and in good spirits. When Goebbels arrived at the Wolf's Lair on 22 July he was deeply moved by Hitler's appearance. The Propaganda Minister was shown the conference hut in which the assassination attempt took place. Trampling over the wreckage, Hitler became extremely agitated by the whole scene and emphasized that there would be vengeance on the treacherous generals that were accomplices in the bomb plot and the attempted military coup that followed. For years, he said, he had held the generals in contempt, particularly his General Staff, for their inability to fight the War properly. He said that the assassination attempt had finally given him an excuse to exterminate, root and branch, the whole clan of generals who were still opposed to him. In this way, he added, he could continue the War with those he trusted, and perhaps begin to turn around its course in Germany's favour.

Already, Hitler's thirst for revenge on the perpetrators was obvious to those living and working at the Wolf's Lair. Each day, it seemed the list of the conspirators grew, causing many at the headquarters, particularly the General Staff, concern. Virtually every section head of the Army General Staff appeared to be implicated. Those that had not already committed suicide were arrested and interrogated, thus providing new names to be added to the long list of suspects. Hitler was handed three names on the arrest list that he never ever expected – Franz Halder, Admiral Canaris and Dr Hjalmer Schacht, pre-war governor of the *Reichbank*. At first he could not believe that such high ranking people were involved. It was a terrible disappointment to him and something that he never got over. In his tormented mind treachery and treason now became the only explanation for his string of military defeats.

Hitler had always been suspicious, but now his suspicions had become obsessions. He trusted nobody but himself, and projected the blame for everything that went wrong on his generals. Even some of his closest collaborators were under suspicion. Everyone now entering the Führer's presence was meticulously scrutinized and all briefcases checked. It was now being considered whether an X-ray screening device should be set up. Warlimont was so angry about having his briefcase checked that he no longer brought it into conference. Many other officers too found the security precautions intimidating or extreme. When they entered the Führer's zone in Security Zone I they found an even greater number than ever before of SS and RSD officers guarding the situation hut and the guest bunker. Even Hitler's food was tested for poison. On one occasion when Marshal Antonescu sent him caviar and sweets he ordered them to be destroyed, fearing they might be poisoned. He even ordered Stauffenburg's executed corpse and others shot by firing squad in Berlin to be cremated, just in case the army had deceived him about their executions. In the eyes of the generals it was worse than the Stalingrad crises. Everyone that entered the Wolf's Lair could feel the grim atmosphere and no one felt safe.

Although the Todt workers knew that they were not under any suspicion, they found that every SS and RSD officer guarding the compound scrutinized their every movement. Ludwik Stanislaw was a Polish labourer who had been contracted to work at the installation on the final phase of its construction. He vividly remembered being searched almost daily and felt that all eyes were on him whenever he moved around the building site. When the final whistle was blown signifying the end of his shift a number of well armed guards immediately came to the fenced-off area which divided the building site from the rest of the security zone. Here the guards watched everyone packing their belongings and scrutinized all workers as they boarded the column of lorries, ready to take them out of the Wolf's Lair. Once they were all herded inside they were escorted out by armoured vehicles accompanied by motorcycle combinations with machine-guns at the ready. At each gate the driver was asked for his special pass and papers, before finally driving out of the last gate at Security Zone IV.

Upon their return next day, the whole process was repeated, but depending upon which officers were at the particular gate, the driver was sometimes searched and all those onboard, as well as the interior of the vehicle. It had been proposed that the workers were to draw up a list of all tools and supplies that they were bringing into the headquarters, and this would be randomly checked by the guards before they entered the headquarters. However, this security measure was never enacted.

Life for everyone at the headquarters had changed forever. Hitler had become a virtual recluse and was very rarely seen wandering around his Security Zone, preferring now to sit in his bunker and brood. To make matters worse, his insomnia became unbearable and he only managed three or four hours sleep in the morning after a heavy dose of sedative. This consequently made him more irritable and bad tempered. Slowly he began to withdraw, not just from the military, but from almost everyone. His secretaries and dog seemed exempt from being accused of treachery and treason. Only they, he repeatedly said, were faithful to him.

During this anxious time, Göring and other equally faithful members did what they could to restore Hitler's trust. A staff stenographer noted in his diary that before the noon conference the *Reichsmarshal* delivered a short speech to the Führer and proposed that as a form of allegiance after the assassination attempt, the entire Wehrmacht should adopt the Hitler salute.

The next day, 24 July, the Hitler salute was made compulsory in place of the old military salute. General Guderian, the newly appointed chief of the General Staff, did what he could to instil belief in National Socialism into the army and try and bring about some kind of accord between it and the party. As a sign of the army's unwavering loyalty to the Führer, he issued two orders of the day assuring Hitler of the Wehrmacht's everlasting devotion and determination to win ultimate victory. The reaction the orders caused throughout the Wehrmacht amazed many members of staff at the headquarters. Even sacked army officers, fearful that they might be suspected of having lost faith in the Führer, or worse still, be suspected of the least sympathy with the plotters, rushed out of retirement to the Wolf's Lair to personally assure Hitler of their absolute allegiance. Even Field Marshal von Brauchitsch, whom Hitler had branded as the root cause of all his troubles in Russia in 1941, and Grand Admiral Raeder, came to the headquarters to emphasize their everlasting and fierce admiration for the Führer and condemn the plotters. They also welcomed the appointment of Himmler as Chief of the Replacement Army, in spite of the fact that they had repeatedly criticized him in the past.

By the summer of 1944, Hitler had reduced his generals into a sad group of frightened and anxious men. There was no more opposition to him whatsoever, not even any criticism. Over the days that followed, the General Staff were lectured repeatedly on how the War on all fronts would be conducted. At the situation conferences they would have to sit there and listen while Hitler moved the fate of entire armies from one part of the map to another. The General Staff did continue at these conferences to voice their own opinions on strategy, movement of the forces and supply, but never to argue with the Führer if he overrode their decision or ideas.

During the last days of July, Hitler's insomnia had become so bad that Dr Giesing recommended cancellation of the nightly tea session. On numerous occasions Hitler admitted that he had tried avoiding staying up half the night in the company of his intimate circle, but he found that it only made his sleep more difficult. He wearily declared that he needed to relax more and stop thinking about the War. Whilst lying on his bunk he could draw an almost exact map of each army group position. This would go around in his head for hours until he finally fell asleep. He was well aware that his life at the Wolf's Lair was making him ill and he needed to change his habits. The assassination attempt of course did nothing to ease the way he felt; nor did his growing concern about losing France.

As the Allies fought across France against the well dug-in and experienced German troops, Hitler was prepared for the worst. Already he and his staff had drafted an order for the 'West Wall' fortifications to be prepared for the defence of the homeland. OKW were instructed to build strong garrisons. As another example of the Führer's growing paranoia, Hitler stipulated that Army Group West headquarters were to be given no information concerning these preparations, as he feared there were still traitors fighting in France corrupting operations.

By early August it was clear that the battle of France was going to be lost. Much of the conference was taken up with consideration of how to avoid utter collapse in the West. Warlimont and others beleived that an immediate withdrawal from France altogether was the best option. Jodl wanted a more gradual strategic withdrawal, stating that a retreat from the coastal sector would be better. Hitler expressed the desire to quit the Wolf's Lair and go to the Western Front to take personal charge, but Eicken and Giesing forbade it. Confined to his Eastern Front headquarters, the Führer was obliged to watch from a distance as the Allies broke out of the Normandy beach head.

On the Eastern Front the situation reports confirmed a far bleaker picture. Throughout July, German troops had been withdrawing steadily through Poland, the weary soldiers forced back by overwhelming enemy pressure. The last of the German infantry units capable of retreating along the Warsaw highway over the Vistula River at Siedlce were Hitler's crack Waffen-SS division *Totenkopf* and the Luftwaffe's Hermann Göring Division. The German position in the East was now cracking, and any hope of repairing it was made almost impossible by crippling shortages of troops. German infantry divisions continued desperately to try to fill the dwindling ranks. However, by early August the Red Army was already making good progress towards the Polish capital, Warsaw. On 7 August, the Soviet offensive finally came to a halt east of Warsaw. Model cabled the Wolf's Lair and gave Hitler an optimistic report that Army Group Centre had finally sent up a continuous front from the south of Shaulyay to the right boundary on the Vistula near Pulawy. The new front in Poland stretched some 420 miles and was manned by 39 divisions and brigades. Although the strength seemed impressive, Hitler knew that the army was weak and thinly stretched. What made matters worse was that reports confirmed that it faced a Russian force that was a third of the total Red Army strength. With these under-strength divisions, the Germans were compelled to hold large areas along the Vistula, which included Warsaw. In Hitler's eyes, Warsaw possessed great strategic importance owing to vital traffic arteries running north–south and east–west, which crossed into the city. Hitler was determined – if he hoped to keep control of the Eastern Front – to hold onto the city at all costs.

The fear of losing the war in the East was bad enough, but to actually see a Russian invasion of East Prussia or Upper Silesia, was a worry that constantly gnawed at Hitler. Troops had already been ordered to renovate the meagre frontier defences and install them with minefields and a motley collection of captured flak and artillery guns. Hundreds of thousands of men and women began frantically digging anti-tank trenches across miles of farmland.

In order to brace the population of East Prussia against the advancing Red Army, Hitler decided to call his Gauleiters to the Wolf's Lair on 4 August. A stooping Hitler greeted the Gauleiters outside the *Führerbunker*. He went from man to man shaking hands. Many, like Friedrich Karl Florian of Düsseldorf, were moved by the sight of their beloved Führer. Although they were rejuvenated by his presence they could see that he was in bad health. After Hitler's impassioned speech to the Gauleiters, a one pot meal was served, after which Hitler slowly staggered to his feet and left the building, trying to hide his stoop.

At the Wolf's Lair, the disaster that was looming in Normandy was openly blamed on the Luftwaffe. Hitler had not seen Göring since 23 July, but the *Reichsmarshal* had for sometime not been welcome at the headquarters to many of the staff. At nearly every conference, for hours on end, officers had to bear the brunt of Hitler's attacks on Göring and what he saw as a corrupt air staff. Göring's advisors were also blamed for lying and making too many hollow promises. As a result of their incompetence, he remarked, the skies over Normandy were virtually defenceless.

To make matters worse, Hans Pfeiffer, Hitler's old adjutant, was killed in a blazing tank in Normandy. If this was not enough, Hans Junge, the young *SS-Hauptsturmführer* who had been his orderly, was killed by a strafing Spitfire. His wife was Hitler's youngest secretary, Traudl Junge. Hitler was so distraught when he heard the news that he kept it a secret until he felt strong enough to tell her in person. But at one midday meal Truadl noticed that he was acting strangely. He said not a word to her and when their eyes met they looked serious and probing. Later in the day, Herman Fegelein telephoned and asked if she could come to his barracks. Comforting her in a fatherly way he slowly broke the news that her husband had been killed in action. The Chief, he said, had known about it since yesterday but was unable to break the tragic news. That evening she was summoned to the

Führer's study. Taking her hands in his Hitler softly spoke and told her how sorry he was about the loss of Hans. He was a fine character, he remarked. He then asked if Traudl would remain his loyal secretary and promised he would always help her.

By 14 August this gloomy episode had been overtaken by events transpiring in France. Tense drama gripped the midday conference as it became clear that France would soon be lost. Out on the battlefield both the Wehrmacht and Waffen-SS were disintegrating. Corps and divisions remained in action on paper, but they were becoming a collection of small battle groups, shrinking down to battalion size.

As the Americans broke out, and the Normandy campaign became mobile, catastrophe threatened. To save the German forces in Normandy from being completely encircled and annihilated, a series of withdrawals had been approved from the Wolf's Lair, which were made through the Falaise–Argentan gap. Hitler and his war staff watched nervously the ominous signs of an army struggling to escape the pending slaughter.

Hitler and OKW were vexed by the outcome in France and fixed the blame upon Field Marshal von Kluge's tactics in Normandy. There were also worrying rumours that Kluge had been consciously misleading the war staff at the Wolf's Lair. Later in the day further evidence convinced Hitler that Kluge was a defeatist and probably anti-Nazi. Another Western Front Field Marshal that Hitler suspected of deliberately ruining the general strategy in France was none other than Field Marshal Erwin Rommel.

The next day the war conference was tense, and those that participated were well aware that Hitler was in a black mood. The conference opened with the normal routine of listening to the daily war reports, and making amendments to the maps. It was confirmed that on 16 August German forces on the Western Front were continuing their retreat by crossing the River Orne. The 12th SS Panzer-Division *Hitlerjugend* desperately battled to keep open the gap. The bulk of the German armour, however, was still trapped in what became known as the Falaise Pocket. Angrily, Hitler remarked that much of his armour would soon be destroyed, and he began to lose his composure. Talking about both the Eastern and Western Fronts, General Guderian remarked that the bravery of the Panzer forces was not enough to make up for the failure of the Luftwaffe and Navy. Suddenly the room went silent. Hitler saw Guderian's comments as defeatist and became even more infuriated. His eyes bulged, and in an effort to contain himself he quickly moved to another room to speak with Guderian. Within minutes their voices became so loud that an adjutant had to caution the Führer that every word could be heard outside the window.

This rage, however, was nothing compared to the one during the evening conference. Hitler had learned that Kluge had disappeared from his post in the West. Either he had been killed in action, or had deserted his post and was negotiating with the enemy. Later that day, a report reached the headquarters that Kluge had arrived to confer with General Hausser and Eberbach in the Falaise Pocket, but there was no explanation of where he had been for the last twelve hours. Hitler could no longer trust Kluge and radioed an urgent message that the Field Marshal was to leave the danger area imminently and direct the rest of the battle from the headquarters of the 5th Panzer Army. General Hausser was instructed to take charge of all forces inside the pocket. Model, who had only just returned to the Eastern Front was called back to the Wolf's Lair and secretly appointed Kluge's successor. He was then sent by aircraft to Kluge with a sealed letter from the Führer ordering him back to Germany. On 20 August, Hitler received news that Kluge was dead, having been killed by a cerebral haemorrhage, according to the army doctor.★

With the death of Kluge, Hitler turned his attention to matters in France, which were now spiralling out of control. To avert a complete catastrophe, Model had been given freedom to evacuate as rapidly as possible units from the Falaise Pocket. Of the 100,000 men breaking out, it was confirmed that some 10,000 were killed and 40,000 captured. Half of them, however, escaped. Hausser was seriously wounded in the attempt, as was General Eugen Meindl. The losses in equipment were appalling and a devastating setback. Some 344 tanks, self-propelled guns, and armoured vehicles, 2,447 motorized vehicles, 252 towed guns, and thousands of horse-drawn vehicles and horses were lost. Approximately 50,000 troops of the Western Front had escaped the slaughter; these troops would no longer be defending France, but the borders of the Reich.

Five days later word reached the Wolf's Lair that Paris had fallen. With the loss of France, Germany's allies began deserting Hitler. The Rumanians declared war on Germany and Finland, Bulgaria and Hungary began defecting. Morale at the Wolf's Lair plummeted to an all time low. Hitler's staff noticed how detached their Führer had become and his trusted secretaries were not even invited for afternoon tea. Tension and drama

---

★ Kluge was under no illusion about what was in store for him when he arrived back in Germany. On 19 August he told his driver to stop the car at Metz, the scene of some of his First World War battles. Here he spread out a blanket and quietly took a cyanide capsule. He left a farewell letter to the Führer, who read it without emotion.

continued to grip the headquarters and the summer heat did nothing to lessen the oppression and despondency everyone felt.

During this period, Hitler excoriated his generals for the string of defeats on both the Eastern and Western Fronts. He branded the General Staff incompetent, and scathingly said that they had failed to ardently believe in final victory.

At the war conference a number of heated debates continued to escalate, with Hitler regularly losing his composure with his generals. In the East the familiar problems made everyone increasingly anxious, especially those that had to listen to their Führer's constant insults and criticism of the way his generals were conducting the War. Soviet forces were already seriously threatening East Prussia and the headquarters staff could occasionally hear the distant rumbling of heavy artillery pounding positions. The approach of the Russians emphasized to everyone at the Wolf's Lair how important it was to infuse the German soldier at the front with iron will and fortitude. With the war in the East taking on a new, more frightening dimension, the situation conferences dragged on longer as Hitler grappled over divisions, trying to plug the huge holes along the front punched in by massive Soviet forces. In southern Poland the 1st Ukrainian Front had captured Lemberg, while Rumania fell to the 2nd and 3rd Ukrainian Fronts. Soviet forces had also penetrated Hungary and its powerful German defences, and the Red Army reached the Bulgarian border on 1 September.

With every defeat Hitler's health took a turn for the worse. Although he was generally seen, according to his secretaries, joking about his right hand, which trembled so much he could no longer shave himself, his physical condition had seriously deteriorated further. His memory too was fading and he easily forgot names and faces.

In early September, Hitler did try and reduce his medication to one injection every day. But yet again within days he was having trouble sleeping. He told Morell he would lay on his bunk unable to sleep with agonising stomach pains. His insomnia was aggravated by the banging and grinding of pneumatic drills used around the clock by the Todt workers in a frantic effort to strengthen the bunkers.

Unwell and tired, Hitler continued to attend the war conferences. On 8 September, Bulgaria and Rumania declared war on Germany. It seemed that nothing but a series of defeats characterised the Eastern Front during that summer of 1944. In a radical effort to stem the series of reverses, General Guderian proposed that 30 divisions of Army Group North, which were stationed redundant in Kurland, be shipped back to the Homeland so that they could be re-supplied and strengthened to reinforce Army Group Centre in Poland. Hitler, however, emphatically rejected Guderian's proposal.

Over the next few days, Hitler watched as the German Army defended Poland with everything it could muster. Reports established that the front lines were being held in many places, making Hitler even more determined to hold out at all costs.

Whilst resolute German forces battled to prevent Red Army troops from spilling out through western Poland and reaching the frontiers of the Reich, Hitler began contemplating a bold plan in the West. Around 12 September he called Jodl to his bunker, who came equipped with a map, which they spread out on Hitler's bedspread. Excitedly, Hitler told a surprised Jodl that he had thought not of another defensive line, but a new offensive, this time against the West.

He said that they were to prepare for a great winter counter-attack through the Ardennes that would mean the capture of Antwerp. He was sure that by sending his powerful Panzers through the Ardennes, as he had done in the summer of 1940, that victory would be secured. Fog and snow would hamper Allied operations and he predicted that the strategic port of Antwerp was within his grasp. With Antwerp lost, he said, the British and Americans would be doomed. A new Dunkirk would emerge, but this time the enemy would be destroyed.

Although the proposal seemed adventurous to his war staff, they thought that the Führer was once more exhibiting an energy and enthusiasm that he had not shown for some time. Many believed that this was the dynamic Hitler of 1940.

By 16 September, American troops were reported to be standing on German soil, and a bloody battle for Aachen, the first big German city under siege, ensued. From the Wolf's Lair Hitler issued a secret message to his commanders, urging them to pass a message to the troops, calling on them for the last-ditch defence of the Reich.

The following day, the headquarters was again inundated by dramatic news. The Allies, it had been reported, instead of attempting a direct assault on the West Wall, had suddenly launched a surprise airborne attack on the key river bridges in Holland. Thankfully for Hitler and his war staff, the attack was a complete failure. Yet during one of the evening conferences Hitler thundered at his generals for allowing the enemy to capture the bridges at Nijmegen intact.

A couple of days later Hitler's anger intensified when he threw himself into a tirade about the Luftwaffe. On 19 September, Göring was called back to the Wolf's Lair and the *Reichsmarshal* had to listen reluctantly to his Führer's biting criticism of the way the Luftwaffe was run. After the discussion Hitler felt ill and seriously considered replacing Göring by a frontline commander like General von Greim. Instead he sacked acting Chief of Air Staff, General Werner Keipe, whom he denounced as a typical self-centred staff officer – a defeatist who was constantly fully of objections. Shortly after midnight, Fegelein told Kreipe that he was to pack his belongings and was forbidden to set foot in the Wolf's Lair again.

Hitler's irrational behaviour during these uncertain times was certainly related to his poor health. Late in the afternoon of the 19th, with a splitting headache, he was driven to the field hospital under heavy guard with a string of armoured vehicles flanked by motorcycle combinations with machine-guns at the ready. When he arrived the whole area was cordoned off and he was escorted into the X-ray room, which had been searched carefully for hidden explosives.

After he was examined he shook hands with the Catholic nursing sisters, and then was given a guided tour by his doctor, Hasselbach, around the wards where his wounded officers of 20 July lay. By this time Schmundt had a high fever, gangrene had set in and he was dying. At the General's bedside, Hitler was seen to be very emotional and on the point of tears. When he rejoined his car his spirits were momentarily lifted by the hundreds of people outside, including recuperating soldiers who had been taking walks in the hospital grounds, some of them on crutches and many with missing limbs. To the astonishment of the guards Hitler stopped and took time to speak with them. Under the spotlight of a number of cameras he was captured even shaking hands and smiling with several wounded soldiers. This was the Hitler of the early years of victory. As he clambered back into his Mercedes the crowds shouted their support with cheers of '*Seig heil!*' For many it was the first time they had ever seen him, and unknown to them, it was probably the last.

Over the next few days Hitler's health became much worse. He again complained of stomach cramps, which were agonizing. In daylight his staff noticed that his skin and eyes had turned an unhealthy yellow. Those who wandered through the grounds of the Führer's restricted zone and managed to get a good glimpse of him were shocked at his appearance. General Nikolaus von Vormann, who visited the Wolf's Lair on 26 September on his way home from the Eastern Front, wrote that Hitler looked tired and broken. He shuffled over to him with drooping shoulders and sat down like an old man. He spoke so softly that it was difficult to understand him.

That evening, Hitler was again racked with terrible stomach cramps. They were so bad that next morning he was unable to get out of bed. Wearing a grey flannel dressing gown over his night shirt, he lay on his bunk; pale, weak and hardly able to bring his voice above a whisper. His staff were shocked by this sudden deterioration in health. No one could remember the Führer being so ill that he could not get out of bed. Some believed he would never recover.

According to Morell's diary, between 28 and 30 September Hitler lost some six pounds and during this period stayed in bed with stomach pains. He was so unwell that the daily war conferences were cancelled. Instead, Admiral Puttkamer, still recovering from his bomb injuries, hobbled in to Hitler's bunker on crutches to read the daily war reports. Puttkamer later remarked that the Führer just lay there not saying a word. Gunsche told Traudl Junge that he had never seen the chief so listless and expressionless. Even the dramatic events unfolding on the Eastern Front failed to animate or interest him.

Occasionally his secretaries would bring him freshly picked flowers and tried to lift his spirits, but it was clear to Traudl Junge that he was very weak and feeble and unable to interact as he normally did in female company. For Traudl and the rest of his intimate staff there was a feeling of despair. They felt that their Führer had given up.

On 1 October, Schmundt died of his injuries from Stauffenberg's bomb. Hitler's adjutant, Richard Schulz, found him sitting on the edge of his bunk in black trousers and a collarless shirt. It was Schulz's 30th birthday and Hitler felt strong enough to present him with the now customary *Glashutte* gold watch.

Over the next few days Morell saw a slight improvement in Hitler's health. Morell was eager for the Führer to leave the confines of his badly ventilated bunker for the clear mountain air of the Berghof, even for a couple of weeks. But in spite of the unsuitability of his bunker with its tiny living and sleeping quarters, and a ventilation system that was inadequate, Hitler was resolute that he did not want to leave the Wolf's Lair, fearing that without his leadership East Prussia would be overrun by the Red Army. Instead, Hitler would direct the War against the East from his headquarters, in spite of his declining health.

Although everyone at the headquarters had been extremely concerned about Hitler's physical condition, doctors Giesing and Brandt both blamed Morell for Hitler's ailments. They agreed that since Stalingrad, Hitler was slowly being poisoned by his little doctor's drugs. These rumours soon became common knowledge around the headquarters and people started whispering that Morell had treated the Führer negligently. Few in Hitler's intimate circle ever believed that Morell had deliberately attempted to poison the Führer. Most of them held Gerda Christinas's opinion that Morell was a good doctor, in spite of his rather shabby appearance. Hitler declared that the rumours were untrue and reassured his faithful doctor that he was not to blame. As a consequence of the rumours he had Morell's rival doctors formally dismissed from the Wolf's Lair. On 9 October Himmler's personal doctor, a 36-year-old orthopedic surgeon named Dr Ludwig Stumpfegger replaced Brandt, Hasselbach and Giesing on Hitler's personal staff.

During Hitler's two-week illness the War stagnated. By 7 October in Poland Army Group Centre, the 3rd Panzer Army and 4th Army were defending a weak salient in the north. To the south-west, the 2nd Army was holding along the River Narew. Army Group A - which would swiftly collapse under the shock of the Soviet avalanche in the New Year - had prepared defences from Modlin to Kaschau. The 9th Army was either side of Warsaw along the Vistula. (It too would be crushed by the Soviet 47th and 61st Armies in January.) The 4th Panzer Army had dug-in at Baranov and was holding out against strong Russian attacks. The 17th Army had prepared a string of machine-gun posts and mines between the Vistula and the Beskides. The 1st Panzer Army was holding Kaschau and Jaslo.

Over the days to come the German Army defended Poland with everything they could muster. The fighting withdrawal had left the bulk of the forces exhausted and undermanned. With reserves almost non-existent the dwindling ranks were bolstered by old men and low-grade troops. Convalescents and the medically unfit were drafted in to what were known as 'stomach' and 'ear' battalions because most men were hard of hearing or suffered from ulcers. Poland would be defended at all costs. It was at this time that Hitler decided that the Varsovians should be punished further for the Warsaw Uprising. Despite the desperate strain on resources, he ordered that what remained of the city be razed to the ground, district by district, building by building.

As Hitler and his war staff braced themselves for the final defence of Poland, news that East Prussia might be threatened became a real cause for concern for everyone at the Wolf's Lair. The East Prussian border was less than 100 miles away from Russian territory and advanced units of the Red Army were reported to be less than 200 miles to the east. Hitler did not hide how grave the situation had become, and geographically his Eastern Front headquarters was now under serious threat from an enemy attack. In anticipation of the battle of East Prussia, he decided it would be safer if he moved over into his newly completed bunker. First, the bunker's gas filtering system, which was installed just in case it came under gas attack, was found to be defective and would have to be fixed, as it was generally believed there was a danger of being gassed by the enemy.

On 16 October, two days after Rommel's death,* the Red Army suddenly stormed into East Prussia evidently forming a spearhead pointed toward the ancient Germanic coastal city of Konigsberg. It was reported that German divisions were outnumbered 4:1. Whilst the Red Army Air Force dived and bombed, on the ground Russian artillery simultaneously pounded the German lines, to a depth of more than three miles in some places. Slowly and systematically the Russians bulldozed their way through, with German troops either fighting to the death, or saving themselves by escaping the slaughter by withdrawing to another makeshift position. The military situation was becoming increasingly desperate. Whilst many areas of the front simply cracked under the sheer weight of the Russian drive, a number of German units continued to demonstrate their ability to defend the most hazardous positions against well-prepared and superior enemy forces. German infantry bitterly contested large areas of countryside. Fighting was often savage, resulting in terrible casualties on both sides; it was also confusing and German communication between the various commands was repeatedly lost, making the situation much worse. As a result, often commanders in the field could not give a precise situation report and this led to numerous problems for the Wolf's Lair. Communication was so bad in some areas that troops that had been embroiled in heavy contact with the enemy for long periods repeatedly found that their rear positions had already been evacuated. As a result, the troops were regularly exposed to heavy fire without support, and on many occasions were quickly encircled and destroyed.

By 22 October it had been confirmed that hundreds of Red Army tanks were heading across northern areas of East Prussia and literally smashing to pieces any German defensive positions that fell in their way. Both night and day the staff could hear the distressing sounds of heavy artillery rolling across the countryside as their brave troops tried in vain to halt the enemy

---

* Rommel in fact had been forced to take cyanide after Hitler had become convinced he was an accomplice in the 20 July bomb plot. The official story of Rommel's death was that Rommel had either suffered a heart attack or succumbed to his injuries from the earlier strafing of his staff car whilst in northern France in July 1944. To give the story credibility, Hitler ordered an official day of mourning in commemoration, and Rommel was buried with full military honours.

advance. Many feared that one day they would suddenly awaken to fighting outside their huts and bunkers. No one could relax. Keitel came over to the *Führerbunker* and asked Hitler to leave for Berlin at once. Martin Bormann secretly ordered the stenographers to begin packing for the move to the chancellery. Others, including Hitler's secretaries, began contemplating packing their suitcases and wanted to know if they would soon be leaving with the Führer. Officers and a number of party officials eager to leave made a variety of excuses as to why they were needed in Berlin. In spite of the fear of the approaching enemy, the Todt workers continued working around the clock reinforcing the installation. Ludwik Stanislaw was quite aware, as were many of his colleagues, that the Wolf's Lair was under threat, but the order from the site foreman was to continue working regardless of the military situation.

Hitler, to the astonishment of his staff, was determined to stay. But he was still far from well and half the evening conferences were cancelled so that he could retire to bed. Many now believed that without his leadership in good health the enemy would soon be at the door. Constant anxiety continued to grip everyone at the headquarters, including many of the generals, who were all in agreement that it would be safer to return to Germany. A number of stories had reached the headquarters that the Soviet advance through East Prussia had been a barbaric one. The Soviets, it seemed, were determined to exact vengeance. These 'slant-eyed Mongols' had butchered women and children. Innocent people had been burned to death with flamethrowers, whilst others were forced to walk naked through the streets, and other less fortunate victims it was rumoured had their tongues nailed to tables, or were hanged from lamp posts. The staff at the Wolf's Lair were appalled at the prospect of being captured, tortured and murdered.

On 23 October there was a sigh of relief when it was announced at the situation conference that the German 4th Army had launched a courageous counter-attack, halting the Russian onslaught through East Prussia. Two days later Hitler told Bormann he would not leave the headquarters until the crisis on the Eastern Front was mastered. His staff nervously resigned themselves to stay with their Führer and watch the battle unfold before their eyes. The female secretaries asked if they should learn to use a gun, but Hitler replied with a warm smile that he had no yearning to die at the hands of one of his secretaries. He assured them that everyone at the headquarters would be safe and he concluded that the enemy would eventually be destroyed.

Hitler was well aware of the grave position, but surprisingly he still showed glimmers of optimism. His great winter offensive gamble in the Ardennes now depended entirely on the Eastern Front remaining stable. From his bunker bedroom he sat for hours with Jodl surveying the first drafts of the plan of attack. To ensure absolute secrecy only a handful of the party faithful were told of the daring offensive. Hitler specifically instructed that under no circumstances would any officers be allowed to speak about the plans, nor were they allowed to teletype or telephone. Only special couriers could pass details of the offensive.

The offensive was undoubtedly a huge risk, but Hitler's military advisors knew they had no choice. During the situation conferences held on the offensive, it was evident to the war staff that Hitler had not lost his nerve in the face of adversity. On 10 November he signed an order to prepare for the Ardennes offensive.

Two days earlier, during the afternoon he had in fact moved over to his newly completed bunker. His sleeping and working quarters were far larger and there were no draughts. After weeks of constant complications with the U-boat type air circulation system, technicians declared the unit safe for use, and the air conditioning system was found not to be dangerous. Herman Giesler, Hitler's Munich architect, visited Hitler in his new bunker and recalled that his bedroom was a windowless cell. Beside his bed there was a low table with a pile of reports, maps, a few books and a telephone. The light from the lamp revealed the dark and dreary concrete walls, which appeared to him like a burial chamber. The restricted sleeping quarters was equipped with a built-in washbasin and fresh air equipment, as well as furniture in natural wood, and he also had his own lavatory. His bed was a simple army cot.

In the morning, Hitler worked in a spacious outer room which could be used as a conference room as well as a dining area. The room had large windows and a nice view of the forest and meadows. But in spite of his new reinforced bunker he was still a prisoner. Visitors were astonished to see him propped up on his spare cot, pale and weak. His breathing was heavy and he appeared to sweat profusely when he moved feebly like an old man from one part of the room to another. Before the conferences, Morell had to now administer a host of drugs, just to get him through the session with his war staff. These were very difficult times for the Führer but he was compelled to oversee all military operations. He blieved that he dare not leave the War in the hands of his generals for one moment.

As the winter closed in on the headquarters, various party officials and generals continued visiting the Führer. Despondent though he may have appeared during these cold, dark days, Hitler was not to show any signs of weakness in his determination to fight to the bitter end. Though he was concerned more than ever about East Prussia being totally engulfed by the Red Army, in front of his staff, particularly his secretaries, he tried to dismiss any possibility that the headquarters was under threat.

His optimism was soon crushed at the war conference by further developments in the East. The Russian forces continued their thrust through the Baltic, and although slowed at several points along the way, they were making good progress and seriously threatening to overwhelm the whole of East Prussia. He left the conference late on 17 November deflated, and knew his days at the Wolf's Lair were numbered.

The following day he surprised his staff by telling them that he now had decided to leave the Wolf's Lair so that he was able to watch the Ardennes campaign more closely. He did not admit to anyone that he had been forced from his headquarters by the advancing Red Army. For Hitler, that would have been admitting defeat. His departure from the headquarters was kept very secret. Most of his staff was told that they would be leaving for the Western Front, and were relieved when he gave the impression that he would soon be returning to the Wolf's Lair. The days and weeks of anxiety were gone for those who did not swallow the story and could now leave, hoping they would never have to return. Hitler himself knew that he would never return but he ordered the construction workers to continue as though he would one day come back.

At 3.15 pm on 20 November, amid the noise and clatter of the construction teams as they continued to work on the last bunkers, Hitler and his entourage left the headquarters for the Gorlitz station to board his train *Brandenburg*. Before the train took the Führer to the Western Front, he was advised to make a visit to Berlin first. On board the train he sat in his compartment with all the shades down and the light switched on. Then he joined some of his staff for lunch. By 5.30 am, the train hauled into Berlin's Grunewald station. Hitler and his entourage drove almost immediately across the blitzed Reich capital to the Reich Chancellery. His stay in Berlin was to last only two weeks.

Just two days after his departure from the Wolf's Lair Hitler surprised Keitel by instructing him to make preparations so that the headquarters would not fall into enemy hands intact. A detonation calendar for all the bunkers and huts was drawn up, and within 24 hours of the final order, code-named *Inselsprung*, the destruction could be carried out. Hitler however, could still not bring himself to destroy his Wolf's Lair, and he told Keitel that he yet might return to East Prussia.

At the Wolf's Lair construction continued, despite the pending detonation of the installation. Gas experts continued worrying about the *Führerbunker*, and the headquarters still functioned more or less as it had done in the past when Hitler was away. Reports from the front were still monitored from the Wolf's Lair and deciphered and accordingly dispatched to Hitler's supreme headquarters, currently in Berlin.

At the end of November Hitler told his headquarters staff to prepare for a trip. At 5 pm on 1 December he secretly left Berlin finally bound for the Western Front. At 1 am, under the cover of darkness he switched from the train to a waiting column of cars and drove to the Eagle's Nest, the bunker headquarters built in 1940 at Bad Nauheim 800 ft above sea level. Within hours of his arrival he was back at work. Following an unusually long conference, his generals would note that he appeared extremely optimistic about the fothcoming Ardennes offensive. He reiterated how important winning the offensive was if they stood any chance of gaining the initiative in the East. Even at this stage of the War Hitler still imagined returning to the Wolf's Lair.

On 7 December he approved the final draft of the offensive, which was kept secret. As mentioned previously, the aim of *Unternehmen Wacht am Rhein* (Operation Watch on the Rhine) was to divide the British and American line in half through the Belgian forests of the Ardennes and capture Antwerp, then encircle and hopefully destroy four Allied armies to ensure – at the very least – that the Allies were in a weaker position when the time came for negotiations for peace. To secure this final victory he now called everyone participating in the war conference preceding the Ardennes offensive to sign a document which swore them to secrecy. A few days before the planned attack he finally summoned the troop commanders of the Western Front to confer with him. Having first been relieved of revolvers and briefcases the generals and their staff were first driven about the countryside to confuse their sense of direction, until the column of cars at last halted at the entrance to the extensive system of bunkers that was the Eagle's Nest. They entered this heavily guarded encampment not knowing why they had been summoned.

The generals were all led down through lines formed by SS to Hitler's underground bunker. The Führer sat at a narrow table flanked by Keitel and Jodl. Across were Rundstedt, Model and General Hasso von Manteuffel, who would command the most powerful of the three armies in the offensive. Half the summoned participants in the room had not seen Hitler for many months and were shocked to find 'a stooped figure with a pale and puffy face, hunched in his chair, his hands trembling, and his left arm subject to a violent twitching which he did best to conceal'. An armed bodyguard stood behind every chair.

In a two-hour speech cum lecture to the 60 or so assembled commanders, Hitler revealed to them the political motives for his decision on an all-out offensive in the West. Over the next few days Hitler appeared confident and in high spirits.

On the eve of the attack, Hitler held a final conference and received a welcome forecast of several days of bad weather, which would ground Allied aircraft. That evening he dined with his secretaries and retired to bed at five in the morning. By the time he was awakened at 11.30 am on the 16th, the American lines had crumbled along an 80-mile front. Confusion gripped the bewildered enemy. The atmosphere at the Eagle's Nest was fizzing with excitement. Hitler was delighted by the progress of the offensive, and was found by his staff already in the conference room eagerly scrutinizing the maps, contrary to custom.

On 23 December, the skies over the Ardennes cleared. By day and night the Allied Air Force gradually regained control. Bombing raids on German supply points in the rear were devastatingly effective and the P-47 Thunderbolts started to hit German troops exposed on the roads. One crisp winter morning Hitler was seen outside his blockhouse impassively watching as 2,000 enemy bombers swarmed eastward. Returning to his bunker he seemed to have shut his eyes to the possibility that outright success could not be achieved. His confidence carried over to Christmas, which he celebrated, to the astonishment of many, with a glass of wine. It was the first time Fraulein Schroder had ever seen him indulge himself.

Three days later at a special meeting with his senior commanders, he admitted the situation was desperate, but he had never learned the word 'capitulation', and would pursue his aims to the end.

At the beginning of the New Year he appeared revitalized by the momentary successes of the Ardennes offensive. But the Führer of 1945 was not the man who had set out for Poland in 1939. He had aged, his back was hunched, his face drawn, his voice quavered, his hair was grey and the famous moustache was snow white. Admiral Heinz Asemann wrote that he looked like a senile man. His midday conference now never started before 5 pm. After it, his doctors insisted that he sleep. He would then take frequent strolls in the snow around his bunker, trying to conceal his trembling left hand. Because of this tremor he could now hardly put pen to paper. Since December, a faithful civil servant had been forging his signature on official citations and awards.

On 3 January, the long awaited news finally reached the snow-covered headquarters that the Allies had gone on the counter-offensive. To make matters worse, on 9 January General Guderian once more journeyed across the frozen plains to the *Führerhauptquartiere* to pester Hitler for the third time about the threat of Stalin's big push. Guderian, using maps and diagrams showed Hitler how the distributions of German strength were understood – and a recommendation that East Prussia be evacuated immediately to save Berlin. Hitler suddenly flew into an uncontrolled rage. Throwing down his magnifying glass he angrily labelled the reports completely idiotic and ordered his Chief of Staff to have the man who had made them shut up in a lunatic asylum. Guderian too lost his temper and boldly told his Führer that Gehlen was one of his best General Staff officers and if he wanted him to be sent to a lunatic asylum, then he should have Guderian certified as well. Hitler's flare-up quickly subsided. The Eastern Front, he said, had never before possessed such a strong reserve and praised Guderian for his work. When Guderian likened the Eastern Front to a house of cards, Hitler lectured him, saying that only iron will and fortitude would hold the front.

When Hitler rose at noon on 11 January news reached his bunker that the the Soviet offensive had already begun. In a few days the German Army was engulfed in a storm of fire along the Vistula Front. The Vistula-Oder Operation, the assault westward to the River Oder, involved nearly four million men. By the end of the day on 13 January the offensive had ripped open a breach more than 20 miles wide. The 4th Panzer Army was smashed. Children and old men were being thrown into what was now being called the last bastion of defence for the Reich. In Army Group Vistula the lines of communication had broken. There was no contact between units on the battlefield, battalions were out of touch with their companies, and regiments had no links with their divisions. The Red Army was ripping apart SS *Reichsführer* Heinrich Himmler's Army Group Vistula. The scattered German ran westward towards the Oder or north-westwards into Pomerania.

As the whole front began to retreat, the 9th and 2nd Army's right wing lost contact. General Weiss's 2nd Army tried to stabilize the front between the towns of Thorn and Graudenz, to little strategic effect. The Soviets had soon wrenched open the door to East Prussia.

Shocked by the appalling losses and devastation on the front, Hitler once again expressed his desire to return to the Wolf's Lair and take command of the terrible situation that was now spiralling out of control. The Führer was warned that developments in the East were now so rapid that it was more than probable that East Prussia would soon fall into Soviet hands. Despite this worrying prospect, Hitler had still not given the order for the Wolf's Lair to be blown up, hoping that by some miracle the Red Army flood would be stemmed. He had however, already instructed those left at the headquarters to be evacuated, including the Todt workers. Keitel, whose job it was to monitor the Russian advance through East Prussia, informed Hitler that the Red Army were reported to be within miles of the East Prussian headquarters and that the complex would inevitably fall. Grudgingly, after weeks of hesitation, Hitler finally gave the order to blow up his greatest headquarters of the War. Once the site had been completely evacuated and files and other important data burnt over an eighteen-hour period between 25/26 January, the demolition began, with General Eduard Hauser's pioneer troops sent into blow up the Wolf's Lair bunkers.

Within hours of the headquarters demolition Russian troops had captured Rastenburg and marched into the Gorlitz forest, finding a tall perimeter fence that led into the Wolf's Lair.

Look on my works, ye Mighty …

After the demolition of the Wolf's Lair Hitler remained in Berlin where he resided at the Reich's Chancellery and fought out the rest of the War. It was here that Hitler and his supreme headquarters would spend their final days entombed beneath the Reich Chancellery building in what became known as the *Führerbunker*. When Hitler committed suicide on 30 April, the fortunes of the Führer headquarters were taken and buried in the ruined, charred remains of the Reich Chancellery gardens, with the man who was its architect. With Hitler dead, his companions were killed or captured, although some escaped as anonymous fugitives.

On 2 May 1945, the Russians finally stormed the Reich Chancellery. Hitler once remarked: 'Men and wars come and go, but what is left, are the buildings.' The Chancellery did indeed outlive its architect, but in 1947 this grand columned structure of yellow stucco and grey stone, which had dominated a quarter-mile stretch of the centre of Berlin since 1939, was ripped from its footings and demolished.

As for the *Führerbunker*, its remains were preserved, entombed 50 feet beneath the Chancellery. It would not be until 1988, more than 40 years later, that workman labouring around the clock began demolishing this monolithic tomb of Nazism. From a historical point of view, one cannot help feeling disappointment at the destruction of Hitler's Berlin bunker, as it bore so much significance during the last days of the War. Yet, just 300 miles to the east, the ruins of the Wolf's Lair still stand today as a reminder of Hitler's determination to win the War against the Soviets and of the titanic Russian sacrifice that thwarted his ambitions. People from all over the world visit the Wolf's Lair and through their interest are preserving the foundations for generations to come.

Here they can visit many of the bunker installations that still stand, despite their contorted appearance. Although many of the visitors are impressed by the sheer size of the bunkers, one is also equally impressed at the amount of explosive charge that must have been used to blow large parts of the concrete bunkers apart. Many of the buildings today lay in heaps of rubble, whilst the larger buildings like the *Führerbunker,* Guest bunker and Göring bunker are a gutted ruin, with twisted and cracked walls and huge fragments of protruding steel lying in the undergrowth.

Surrounding the bunkers were the concrete-covered brick barrack-type buildings, which were the most common structure at the Wolf's Lair. Many of these were mined and completely destroyed, whilst some were burnt out and still stand there today intact with their roofs.

The original railway line which passed through the headquarters in the Gorlitz Forest was destroyed during the Wehrmacht's evacuation in January 1945. After the War a single track was laid by the Poles, which now operates only to Angerburg. The walls and foundations of the old brick railway station at the headquarters still stand today, but all other buildings in and around the area were heavily mined and are now piles of twisted rubble.

Despite the undergrowth, the many trees, and the disappearance of many of the paths and roads, Hitler's former headquarters remains a fascinating place to visit. More than 60 years since the Führer vacated the Wolf's Lair for the last time, the appearance of the installation is changing dramatically with every passing decade.

End Notes

1   Diary of Fraulein Christa Schroder [BA/1509/00]
2   Memoirs of Field-Marshal Keitel [manuscript written in prison at Nuremberg NA568432/8/11]
3   Diary of Fraulein Christa Schroder [BA/1511/0]
4   Diary of Fraulein Christa Schroder [BA/1513/A]
5   Diary of Fraulein Christa Schroder [BA/1515/C]
6   OKW diarist Helmuth Greiner diary, summer 1941. Draft entries in the war diary of the National Def Br, Wehrmacht operations [Paper 85137]
7   OKW diarist Helmuth Greiner diary, summer 1941. Draft entries in the war diary of the National Def Br, Wehrmacht operations [Paper 85137]
8   Dr Morell's Treatment Diaries [National Archives]
9   Diary of Fraulein Christa Schroder [BA/15060/41]
10 General Halder War Diary [NA-2586 & KTB-Series]
11 Walther Hewel Diary [Paper ACK/5713]
12 Diary of Fraulein Christa Schroder [BA/15093/63]
13 Walther Hewel Diary [Paper ACK5713]
14 Diary of Fraulein Christa Schroder [BA/15099/69]
15 OKW diarist Helmuth Greiner diary. Draft entries in the war diary of the National Def Br, Wehrmacht operations [Paper 77/157]
16 Paper written by Major Zitzewitz during the battle of Stalingrad [Paper-EDZ/5757/0A]
17 Diary of General Heinz Guderian [NA Microfilm T/78]
18 Diary of Fraulein Christa Schroder [BA/1652/103]
19 Diary of Traudl Humps (Junge) [John Toland, *Adolf Hitler*, Doubleday, 1976 page 552]

20 Diary of Traudl Humps (Junge) [John Toland, *Adolf Hitler*, Doubleday, 1976 page 552]

21 Diary of Traudl Humps (Junge) [John Toland, *Adolf Hitler*, Doubleday, 1976 page 552]

22 Diary of Traudl Humps (Junge) [John Toland, *Adolf Hitler*, Doubleday, 1976 page 552]

23 Dr Morell Treatment Diaries (National Archives)

24 Institute fur Zeitgeschichte, Munich, [MA163-43]

25 Diary of Fraulein Christa Schroder [BA1754/143]

26 NKVD Report – Feb 1945. Moscow Archives [translated from Russian into English for Author]

Appendix A

Russian NVKD Investigative Report on the Wolf's Lair and surrounding area

In February 1945, just three weeks after the Wolf's Lair was blown up, Russian intelligence confirmed in an official report what was found during its investigation of the site. The translated document reads:

Stamp
Special File /-/.s.?92
Copy
Top Secret
Stamp: removed from secret file
The People's Commissar of the interior of USSR
Comrade L P Beria

As it is known to you from numerous operational materials Hitler's headquarters was in East Prussia in the neighbourhood of the town of Rastenburg [now Ketrzyn]. After the occupation of this area by our armies we have undertaken a search for a place where Hitler's military quarters were situated.

With this purpose in view we have taken advantage of the operational materials in our possession as well as disclosures by various arrested men. The result was that on 14 February 1945 in the region of the Masurian Lakes in the triangle between Rastenburg, Lotzen and Angerburg, with the radius of some 50 kilometres a place was found where Hitler had his quarters. There was also found Himmler's headquarters, Ribbentrop's residence, the High Commands of the Land Forces' quarters, and the Hotel 'Hunters' House', where high ranking officers used to stop who had appointments with Hitler. When we were in the location we made a thorough survey of the area and buildings in which Hitler, Himmler and Ribbentrop were staying. We also inspected the quarters of the High Command of German Land Force. The area where Hitler's quarters were situated, included concrete constructions, fences of barbed wired, minefields, a large number of fixed posts made of earth and wood, and an extensive array of well camouflaged emplacements for security guards. The extensive security suggests that the quarters would have been very difficult to penetrate.

1. Hitler's quarters were situated near Rastenburg, in a forest and covered an area of about 4 square kilometres. In the neighbourhood of the quarters, within a 10-kilometre radius extends a forbidden zone. No buildings or inhabitants are there. A road and railway line are leading to the place where Hitler's headquarters were situated. In the territory of the headquarters the ways of access, their borders and vacant ground were all mined. At the entrance to the forest where the quarters are situated, there is the first barrier. On both sides are the inscriptions: 'Stop Military Object. No Admittance to Civilians'. Behind the barrier is an announcement: 'It is forbidden to leave this road. Danger to life. Commanding Officer'. Similar announcements are placed all around the quarter's area. The forest is entirely surrounded on the outside by several rows of barbed wire, among which are obstacles constructed out of twisted wire of the type 'Spirala Bruno'. On the right-hand side of the barrier are some sheds with a large number of mines and camouflaging materials, whereas on the left-hand side are barracks for the soldiers manning the site. At the same place grenades and motor car materials were also kept. Further on, in the depth of the forest stand camouflage watch towers up to the height of 35 metres. On the left- and right-hand sides of the road are access ditches and trenches at a distance of about 1.5 metres from the first barrier. [Further on] there is a second barrier. Nearby is the following inscription: 'The persons who enter this area must report at the Commandant's Guard House'. Beyond the second barrier begins the second ring of wire fences. It is constructed of special iron hoops in several rows which encompass Hitler's headquarters. Apart from the wire fences there was another fence set up with a metal net and topped with barbed wire. Presumably, the fence and the net were conductive to a high tension electric current.

Beyond gate No.1, begins an area occupied by the quarters themselves. It contains up to 12 enormous buildings which the Germans call 'bunkers'. All bunkers have been blown up. Bunkers are concrete buildings erected above the surface and contain ceilings made of rafters. The height of the bunker reaches approximately 14 metres, thickness of its side walls 5 metres, and thickness of concrete ceilings made of rafters may be up to 8 metres. Inside the bunkers were some passages going through. Their width was up to 2 metres. In the bunkers were discovered gaps going down, but it could not be established whether there were any underground constructions since the explosions have filled the gaps with rubble. The concrete buildings – bunkers – were serving as shelters against air-raids ... All bunkers and the other buildings of concrete are painted in the colour of the surrounding forest. Over the surfaces of the bunkers and other buildings are spread special camouflage nets together with artificial trees and bushes placed there. Alleys and roads around the buildings are covered with green camouflage nets. Roads and ways of access to the buildings were lit by navy blue electric lamps with shades.

Beyond the second ring of the wire fences, numerous concrete gun posts and other protective measures extended to the third ring of the wire fences as well as a metal railing surrounding the main part of the quarters in which Hitler presumably resided. Within the third ring of the wire fences a concrete bunker with an adjoining little house is situated. The house has a ground floor only and its window shutters are made of steel plates. Around this building are distributed more than 10 gun posts. Eight metres away from the bunkers is a garage for sixteen motor cars. Having got into the interior that was destroyed as the result of an explosion in the building adjoining the bunker we found a corridor with six rooms on the left side. On the right side of the corridor was one large room only in which apparently conferences were held. In the six rooms were beds and wardrobes; in one of the rooms in the wall was a safe which proved to be empty on opening. The pieces of furniture were simple, beds made of wood and metal, no soft furniture at all. At the end of the corridor were toilets and a special entrance to the bunker. When an air raid was imminent Hitler probably was using this concrete passage in his bunker. The following materials show that Hitler was situated here:

1) On one of the doors of the rooms where Hitler was supposed to stay was the inscription 'Führer's Aide-de-Camp of the Army'.
2) The order issued by the commandant of Hitler's quarters dated 8 January 1945 refers to the necessity of keeping secrets as incumbent on all military personnel employed in this particularly important objective. The order conventionally calls the object 'Wolfschanze', which means translated, 'Wolf's Lair'. We have verified this name with the interpreters and German officers under arrest. The arrested men have confirmed that Hitler's quarters was conventionally called 'Wolf's Lair', and this is a well known fact to the higher ranking officers of the German Army. The term 'Wolfschanze' seems to be connected with a historical origin of the name Adolf, which means 'a brave Wolf' in old Germanic.

3) A Photograph of Hitler and Mussolini with some generals in the quarters. Moreover, we found in the area of Hitler's quarters a list of telephone holders there. Hitler appears on the list as No.1, then follows his ADC, Chief of General Staff etc. A topographical map was also found on which locations of Hitler's headquarters, Himmler's headquarters, the High Command of the Land Forces' quarters, and Ribbentrop's residence were marked. There was also found a document from 'Todt Organization' dated 18th January 1945, with reference to additional building works to be made in the area of Hitler's quarters. Not far from Hitler's building, on the other side of the railway line is a concrete bunker, in which – according to the inscription – a command centre and anti-aircraft staff of Hitler's quarters were stationed.

2. Himmler's headquarters. These occupy an area of approximately four square kilometres, in a forest, at a distance of ten kilometres from the town of Angerburg. A road and railway line leads from Himmler's headquarters to connect them with Hitler's quarters. Around the headquarters for about three kilometres extend three lines of wire fences. The spaces between the fences are mined. Like in Hitler's quarters there is a fence of metal net topped by barbed wire. The fence is surrounded by well camouflaged high watch towers set up on trees. Between the first and second line of the wire fences on all corners, were gun post positions and mines. Between the second and third line of the wire fences were some buildings of concrete, brick and wood, as well as some 20 underground bunkers for Himmler's personal guards. It is known from the documents found that units of the SS were employed here. Along the road of Himmler's quarters were placed inscriptions to the effect that deviation from the road was forbidden and dangerous to life. Within the centre ring of the fences and fence of metal net were 5 concrete bunkers of the same type as in Hitler's quarters, and a whole series of other buildings. All bunkers and buildings were blown up with an exception of one bunker that cracked only as the result of an explosion, but did not crumble into pieces at all. Within the area of Himmler's quarters was a small prison which burnt down, but the five concrete cells inside were still standing. The prison was guarded by a special police battalion whose commander was Major Krumme.

Aside from the bunkers and other buildings some wooden sheds were preserved intact. They were carefully swept, but no documents or notes whatever were left behind and all furniture was taken away. In some rooms straw and bottles of kerosene were found. It is believed that the sheds were intended for destruction by fire.

It is obvious from the materials in hand that during his stay, Himmler in the quarters was living and working in a special train which remained camouflaged in the quarters area. It has been confirmed that in the area of Himmler's quarters there was in fact a branched-off railway line and under close scrutiny it has been suggested that the train could not be seen even at close distance. All access ways to the train were mined along their borders. The side line was surrounded by dense barbed wired. Near the place where the train was stationary were defensive positions.

The camouflaging of the whole of Himmler's quarters was prepared with the same thoroughness as that of Hitler's quarters, and the same materials were used. The transformation cabin through which the electric current was supplied to the quarters was not blown up. A dense net of telephone and telegraph cables was installed at Himmler's quarters.

3. The quarters of the High Command of the German Land Force was situated at a distance of 15 kilometres from the town of Angerburg on the road from Angerburg to Rastenburg on the shore of Lake Mauersee. A road and railway line connected these quarters with the quarters of Hitler and Himmler. A forbidden zone barring any admittance starts at five kilometres before the railway station. At the road there is a large inscription to the effect that the road is closed to civilians between the localities Stobben – Pastdorf. The forest in which the quarters were encompassed consisted of several rows of wire fences. Access ways to those on all sides were mined and the signs around them read: 'Mines'.

In the area of the quarters were placed the same inscriptions as at Hitler's quarters, which warned that deviation from the road was a threat to life. Around the area of the quarters were underground shelters and trenches as well as numerous posts for anti-aircraft artillery. Inside the quarters there were some twenty concrete bunkers of the same type as in Hitler's quarters, but smaller in size. Apart from the bunkers there was a considerable amount of wooden sheds built for habitation. They had brick foundations and they were equipped with central heating and electric lights. The majority of the bunkers were intact. No documents were found inside. In the area of the quarters were a large number of the concrete and earth shelters as well as narrow openings for anti-aircraft artillery. There were some ten watch towers. All buildings and constructions were camouflaged. They conveyed an impression of woodland.

The quarters were connected with a large number of telephone and telegraph cables. In the quarters area of the High Command of the German Land Forces was found correspondence of the General of Engineer units at the General Staff, General Inspector of the Panzer troops, TODT Organization of the General Staff, General Inspector of the Commander-in-Chief of the General Staff, Commanding Headquarters of the Commander-in-Chief of the German Army, Department of Alien Force 'East' and the Chief of Staff of the German Land Forces. It follows from the documents that this was the place where the Commander-in-Chief of the German Land Forces had his quarters.

4. Ribbentrop's residence was situated in the land property of Count Lehndorff at a distance of some 30 kilometres from the town of Rastenburg on the road Rastenburg – Angerburg. It is a one storey brick building with a mansard. The first half of the house was occupied by Ribbentrop with his Foreign Ministry Personnel. Count Lehndorff being a member of a military plot in Germany was shot dead in 1944. Personal guards of Ribbentrop, of which there were 60 men, were distributed in underground shelters and around neighbouring localities. A road with a good surface led from the property to the quarters of Hitler and Himmler.

5. A Hotel called 'The Hunters' Lodge' is situated at a distance of 2 kilometres from the town of Angerburg on the road Angerburg – Lotzen, on the shore of Lake Schwenzeitsee. Documents show that this hotel provided a temporary accommodation for high ranking officers of the German Command who had appointments with Hitler. The hotel is comfortably equipped and has good furniture. Its whole area is surrounded by wiring. Around the fences are access ditches and narrow openings. The camouflage gave the area an impression of a massive forest. In this area were watch towers from which the countryside may be observed with a radius of a few kilometres. There are inscriptions: 'No admittance to civilians. Stop. Motor cars are not allowed to stop longer than two minutes.'

The Hotel is connected with Hitler's quarters by an asphalt road. An airfield is not far from the Hotel. Sentinels from the NKVD units were placed by us in the area occupied by Hitler's quarters and Himmler's quarters, High Command's of the German Land Forces quarters and Ribbentrop's residence.

Our men make a further search for all documents that may be of interest. In my opinion it would be of a matter of interest for our specialists to come to the area of Hitler's quarters to inspect all concrete buildings – bunkers.

Plenipotentiary NKVD USSR at the 3rd Byelorussian Front – Abakumov.

Sent to:
Comrade Stalin
Comrade Molotov
Comrade Malenkov

22nd February 1945
Nr 164/b

For concordance: An. Gumilev.[26]

Appendix B

Prominent Military and Party Officials Appointed to the Wolf's Lair 1941-1944

Oberbefehlshaber der Wehrmacht

General Rudolf Schmundt (Hitler's Chief Adjutant). Seriously wounded by assassination attempt and died on 1 October 1944 in the military hospital at Rastenburg.

General Wilhelm Burdorf (Hitler's Chief Adjutant from 12 October 1944 until 2 May 1945)

General Gerhard Engel (Army Adjutant)

Major Heinrich Borgmann (Army Adjutant)

General Erik von Amsberg (Army Adjutant)

Captain Karl-Jesco von Puttkammer (Naval Adjutant)

Major Nicolaus von Below (Luftwaffe Adjutant)

Lieutenant Willi Johannmeyer (Army Personnel Adjutant)

SS-Major Fritz Darges (Personal Adjutant to Hitler)

SS-Captain Richard Schulz-Kossens (Personal Adjutant to Hitler)

SS-Captain Hans Pfeiffer (Hitler's Escort Command)

SS-Second Lieutenant Heinz Kersten (Führerbegleitkompanie)

SS-First Lieutenant Heinz Linge (Hitler's Personal Servant)

Oberkommando der Wehrmacht OKW

General Field Marshal Wilhelm Keitel (Chief of OKW)

Captain Ernst John von Freyand (Adjutant)

General Alfred Jodl (Chief of Operations)

Lieutenant Colonel Eckhard Christian (Chief of Luftwaffe Operations North)

Major Heinz Waizenegger (General Staff Officer in OKW Operations)

Major Hermann Brudermueller (Operational Section)

General Lieutenant Walter Warlimont (Acting Chief of Operations)

General Lieutenant August Winter (Operations)

Colonel Horst Freiherr Treusch von Buttlar-Brandenfels (General Staff Officer)

Lieutenant Colonel Wilhelm Meyer-Detring (Staff of the Wehrmacht Command)

Captain Wolfe Junge (Staff of the Naval Command)

Captain Heinz Assmann (Staff of the Naval Command)

Lieutenant Colonel Bohm-Tettelbach (Staff of the Luftwaffe Command)

General Walter Buhle (Chief of Army Staff)

Lieutenant Walter Scherff (representative of Hitler for Military History)

First Lieutenant Wilhelm Scheidt (Army Military History)

OKH

General Franz Halder (Chief of Army General Staff until September 1942)

General Kurt Zeitzler (Chief of Army General Staff)

General Adolf Heusinger (acting Chief of Army General Staff from 10 June 1944 through 21 July 1944. Deputy of the Chief of the Army General Staff from 22 July until October 1944)

Major Gunther Smend (Adjutant to the Chief of the Army General Staff)

Major Bernd Freiherr Freytag von Lonringhoven (Operations Section of the Army General Staff from November 1943)

General Walter Wenck (General Staff of the Army from 1 September until February 1945)

First Lieutenant August Hermani (General Staff of the Army)

Major Hubertus Freiherr von Humboldt-Dachroeden (General Staff of the Army, Operations Division)

Lieutenant Colonel Ulrich de Maiziere (Army Operations Officer)

General Wilhelm Burgdorf (Chief of Army Personnel)

General Ernst Maisel (Acting Chief of Army Personnel from October 1944)

General Wolfgang Thomale (Chief of the Staff of the General Inspector of the Panzer Troops)

OKM

Admiral Erich Raeder (Admiral and Chief of the Navy until January 1943)

Admiral Karl Donitz (Admiral and Chief of the Navy from January 1943 until April 1945)

Captain Jan-Heinrich Hansen-Nootbaar (Adjutant to Naval Command)

Admiral Gerhard Wagner (Operations Officer)

Admiral Theodor Krancke (Representative of Naval Command)

Admiral Hans-Erich Voss (Naval Liaison Officer)

OKL

Reich-Marshal Hermann Göring (Commander-in-Chief of Luftwaffe)

Major Bern von Brauchitsch (Chief Adjutant and Adjutant to Göring from January 1943)

General Hans Jeschonnek (Chief of the General Staff of the Luftwaffe)

General Gunther Korten (Chief of the General Staff of the Luftwaffe until died of his wounds after the assassination attempt on 20 July)

General Werner Kreipe (Chief of the General Staff of the Luftwaffe from late July 1944)

General Karl Koller (Acting Chief of the General Staff of the Luftwaffe)

General Hans Jeschonnek (Chief of Luftwaffe Operations)

General Eckhard Christian (Chief of Luftwaffe Operations from September 1944)

General Karl Bodenschatz (Luftwaffe Liaison Officer until badly wounded on 20 July 1944 assassination attempt and unfit for duty)

General Oskar Schuster (Chief of the Weather Service to the Chief of the General Staff of the Luftwaffe)

Reichsführung SS

Reichsführer SS Heinrich Himmler (Commander-in-Chief of the SS)

SS-Obergruppenführer Karl Wolf (Himmler's Personal Staff)

SS-Brigadeführer Hermann Fegelein (Himmler's Liaison Officer)

SS-Hauptsturmführer Johannes Goehler (Adjutant to Hermann Fegelein from August 1944)

Reich Party Members

Martin Ludwig Bormann (Reich Leader and Head of the Party Chancellery)

Joachim von Ribbentrop (Foreign Minister of Germany)

Walther Hewel (Ministerial Director and Permanent Representative of the Foreign Minister to Hitler)

Dr Franz von Sonnleithner (Ministerial Director and acting leader of the Personal Staff of the Foreign Minister)

Professor Albert Speer (Reich Architect and Reich Minister for Armaments and Munitions; Head of the OT, General Inspector for German Roadways and General Inspector for Water and Energy)

Dr Otto Dietrich (Reich Press Chief)

Helmut Sundermann (Deputy Press Chief)

Heinz Lorenz (Adjutant to the Reich Press Chief)

SS-Standartenführer Wilhelm Zander (Staff of the Deputy of the Führer and Reichsleiter Bormann)

Reichssicherheitsdienst – RSD

The RSD was composed mainly of police personnel, highly trained for the main purpose of guarding and protecting Hitler. The RSD were under the command of SS-Brigadeführer Hans Rattenhuber. All members of the RSD wore the standard SS uniform with black unit collar patches, displaying the 'SD' diamond on the lower left sleeve. At the Wolf's Lair the RSD were responsible for guarding and protecting the headquarters inside the perimeter of the installation and ensuring that the Führer's living space and work areas were protected. The FBB were given the duty of guarding the outer perimeter of the headquarters. The following names are some of the RSD personnel that were posted to the Wolf's Lair, which were taken from Himmler's personal files in January 1945.

SS-Untersturmführer Karl Asmus
SS-Untersturmführer Heinrich Bambey
SS-Obersturmführer Friederich Barthel
SS-Hauptsturmführer Joseph Bastian
SS-Brigadeführer and General Major of the Police Hans Baur
SS-Untersturmführer Heinrich Beck
SS-Untersturmführer Paul Berger
SS-Hauptsturmführer Johan Bergmuller
SS-Hauptsturmführer Ludwig Bergmuller
SS-Obersturmführer Georg Betz
SS-Untersturmführer Walter Beyer
SS-Hauptsturmführer Fritz Birzer
SS-Obersturmführer Friedrich Bitter
SS-Untersturmführer Franz Brandenburg
SS-Untersturmführer Stephan Buhler
SS-Untersturmführer Ernst Bunde
SS-Obersturmführer Anton Danner
SS-Untersturmführer Johann Danner
SS-Untersturmführer Johann Driessle
SS-Obersturmführer Wilhelm Eckold
SS-Untersturmführer Leonhard Escofier
SS-Hauptsturmführer Hans Friedrich
SS-Untersturmführer Johann Freitag
SS-Hauptsturmführer Hans Germann (radio operator on Hitler's escort plane)
SS-Untersturmführer Franz Grill
SS-Untersturmführer Hans-Joachim Hassenstein
SS-Hauptsturmführer Paul Heinecke

SS-Sturmbannführer Paul Henke
SS-Obersturmführer Erwin Hinz
SS-Sturmbannführer Peter Hogl (head of Hitler's Personal Guard)
SS-Hauptsturmführer Josef Hosl
SS-Obersturmführer Max Hoffmann
SS-Untersturmführer Werner Hohmann
SS-Untersturmführer Johan Hubinger
SS-Hauptsturmführer Bernhard Hunn
SS-Untersturmführer Walter Ingrish
SS-Untersturmführer Hugo Jaeschke
SS-Untersturmführer Karl Janssen
SS-Hauptsturmführer Josef Jorg
SS-Untersturmführer Christian Kennerknecht
SS-Sturmbannführer Josef Kiermaier
SS-Untersturmführer Anton Knorr
SS-Untersturmführer Karl Kohler
SS-Untersturmführer Walter Korn
SS-Untersturmführer Franz Kratzer
SS-Untersturmführer Kurt Krick
SS-Untersturmführer Kurt Kriebeler
SS-Obersturmführer Johann Kuffner
SS-Obersturmführer Karl Lang
SS-Obersturmführer Heinrich Lauerwald
SS-Obersturmführer Paul Leciejewski
SS-Untersturmführer Nikolaus Lorenz
SS-Hauptsturmführer Paul Leciejewski
SS-Untersturmführer Erich Madsack
SS-Obersturmführer Karl Manthey
SS-Untersturmführer Alfred Maurer
SS-Untersturmführer Paul Meissner
SS-Untersturmführer Karl Meister
SS-Untersturmführer Johann Muller
SS-Untersturmführer Karl Muller
SS-Untersturmführer Alfred Mundt
SS-Untersturmführer Franz Neidel
SS-Hauptsturmführer Hermann Nein
SS-Hauptsturmführer Ernst Noack
SS-Obersturmführer Alois Oppelt
SS-Untersturmführer Johann Ortner
SS-Untersturmführer Sebastian Osterhuber

SS–Untersturmführer Joseph Portner
SS–Brigadeführer Hans Rattenhuber
SS–Untersturmführer Franz Rausch
SS–Hauptsturmführer Werner Ropert
SS–Untersturmführer Wili Roganz
SS–Untersturmführer Anton Schlammer
SS–Untersturmführer Hermann Schlemmer
SS–Untersturmführer Eduard Schmid
SS–Sturmbannführer Konrad Schmidbauer
SS–Sturmbannführer Friedrich Schmidt
SS–Obersturmführer Georg Schmidt
SS–Untersturmführer Johann Schmidt
SS–Untersturmführer Hugo Schneller
SS–Untersturmführer Konrad Scholz
SS–Untersturmführer Karl Schulein
SS–Untersturmführer Paul Schumm
SS–Untersturmführer Martin Schwagler
SS–Obersturmführer Albert Sebald
SS–Untersturmführer Joseph Volk
SS–Untersturmführer Georg Vollnhals
SS–Sturmbannführer Johann Weber
SS–Obersturmführer Karl Weckling
SS–Untersturmführer Hans Windisch
SS–Hauptsturmführer Johann Windorfer
SS–Hauptsturmführer Hans Wolf
SS–Sturmbannführer Ernst Zaske
SS–Untersturmführer Karl Zenger
SS–Obersturmführer Karl Zimmer
SS–Hauptsturmführer Erich Zimmermann
SS–Hauptsturmführer Max Zintel
SS–Untersturmführer Agust Zollner

Appendix C

Composition of the FBB at the Wolf's Lair late 1944

I. Führer-Begleitbataillon (armoured)
  4 Panzergrenadier companies
  1 Panzer company
  1 Flak company
II. Führer-Begleitbataillon (Motorised)
  2 Grenadier companies (Motorised)
  1 assault engineer company
Panzerabteilung (Anti-Aircraft Section)
  7 batteries
Auflarungskompnaie (Reconnaissance Company)

Appendix D

Wolf's Lair Security 1941-1944

Security Zone I
RSD, SS-Begleitkommando
RSD (Rattenhuber Chief of HQ security)
FBB Guards
(Security mainly consisted of FBB guards, but later in the War more SS were used to increase security)

Security Zone II
FBB Guards
RSD, SS-Begleitkommando

Security Zone III & IV
FBB Quarters

III Platoon 2nd Company FBB	Office 1st Company
Guard Platoon 7 FFA	Fire Fighting Company
Search Light Section	Enlisted men, Staff Commandant
Supply Section 1st Company FBB	II Platoon 3rd Company
Special Commando 'W'	III Platoon 3rd Company
1st Company FBB	FBB (Lt Pieper)
Signal Platoon	Officer 3rd Company
I Platoon 1st Company FBB	I Platoon 3rd Company (Lt Wegmann)
I Platoon 1st Company	Guard House West
FBB (2nd Lt Stumpf)	Guard House East
III Platoon 1st Company	Guard House South
FBB (Lt Seidte)	Guard Quarters
Troop Quarters	Guard House I

Sergeant Major Hildebrand
Quarters
Lt Kessel Quarters
II Platoon 1st Company FBB
II Platoon 1st Company FBB

Guard House II
Major Gnass Quarters
Officers Kasino 3rd Company

Throughout the Wolf's Lair installation, guards manned the gun emplacements, bunkers, anti-aircraft gun towers, machine-gun towers, and machine-gun emplacements around the clock. On the outer perimeter of the headquarters there were a number of security guard posts of the FBB. Inside and outside the fences throughout the HQ area there were also telephones, waters taps, foxholes and short trenches, dugouts, munitions depots and minefields. Inside Security Zone III and IV were guard houses, special commandos, quarters, barracks and supplies of the FBB.

Appendix E

SS Weaponry at the Wolf's Lair

Following the assassination attempt on Hitler on 20 July 1944, security at the Wolf's Lair was increased and elements of Hitler's personal bodyguard detachment, the Leibstandarte-SS Adolf Hitler, arrived and occupied all major points inside the compound and sealed off Security Zone I. All SS guards were added to every FBB post inside and outside the headquarters. An entire SS alert unit was employed inside Security Zone I. The bulk of the weapons and equipment used by the Leibstandarte at the Wolf's Lair was more or less identical to that used by the FBB. The Leibstandarte arrived at the headquarters with a large variety of weaponry, everything from small arms to heavy tanks. Below is a list of weaponry stocked by the SS at the Wolf's Lair in 1944.

Small Arms
Pistole 08 Pistol or Luger
Pisztoly 37M Hungarian Service Pistol
Frommer 7.65mm Hungarian Pistol
Model 1914 Norwegian Service Pistol
Maschinenkarabiner 42
Gewehr 41 (W) Self-Loading Rifle
Maschinenpistole (MP) 28
Maschinenpistole (MP) 43
Sturmgewehr 44 (Assault Rifle)
Maschinenpistole (MP) 38
Maschinenpistole (MP) 40
Kar 98K Bolt-Action Rifle

Infantry Support Weapons
Maschinengewehr 34 (MG)
Maschinengewehr 42 (MG)
5cm Leichte Granatwerfer (leGW) 36 Mortar
Flammenwerfer (FlW) 41
Steilhandgrenate 39

Anti-Tank and Anti-Aircraft Weapons
7.92mm Panzerbüsche 38 Anti-Tank Rifle
7.92mm Panzerbüsche 39 Anti-Tank Rifle
3.7cm Pak 35/36 Anti-Tank Gun
5cm Pak 38 Anti-Tank Gun
7.5cm Pak 40 Heavy Anti-Tank Gun
8.8cm Pak 43 Heavy Anti-Tank Gun
Faustpatrone 30 Anti-Tank Rocket
Raketenpanzerbüsche (RPzB) 54 Anti-Tank Rocket Launcher
2cm Flugabwehrkanone (Flak) 30
2cm Flugabwehrkanone (Flak) 38
8.8cm Flugabwehrkanone (Flak) 18

Artillery
10.5cm leFH 18 Light Field Howitzer
7.5cm Leichte Feldkanone 18 (leFK)
7.5cm Feldkanone 40 (FK 40)

Armoured Cars
Sd.Kfz.222
Sd.Kfz.223
Sd.Kfz.231
Sd.Kfz.263

Artillery Prime Mover Halftracks
Sd.Kfz.6
Sd.Kfz.7
Sd.Kfz.8
Sd.Kfz.10

Light Armoured Reconnaissance Halftracks
Sd.Kfz.250 Series

Light Ammunition Carrier Halftrack
Sd.Kfz.252
Sd.Kfz.253

Medium Armoured Personnel Carrier Halftrack
Sd.Kfz.251

Panzers
Pz.Kpfw.III
Pz.Kpfw.IV

Assault Guns and Tank Destroyers
Panzerjäger Marder.III
Panzerjäger Wespe

Appendix F

Hitler's Military Headquarters Movements 1941-1944

1941

24 June 1941: Hitler departed for East Prussia on his special train *Amerika* and was based at Wolf's Lair for the campaign against the Soviet Union.

7 November 1941: Hitler returned to East Prussia and resumed directing the War from the Wolf's Lair.

28 August 1941: Hitler visited Uman by aircraft in the Ukraine with Mussolini to inspect Italian troops fighting on the Eastern Front.

29 August 1941: Hitler returned to East Prussia and resumed directing the War from the Wolf's Lair.

24 September 1941: Hitler flew to Borrisow in Russia to visit Army Group Centre and to confer with Field Marshal von Bock.

26 September: Hitler returned to East Prussia and resumed directing the War from the Wolf's Lair.

2 October 1941: Hitler departed from Wolf's Lair by *Amerika* for Berlin where he delivered a speech about the progress of the campaign in Russia.

4 October: Hitler returned to East Prussia and resumed directing the War from the Wolf's Lair.

7 November 1941: Hitler left the Wolf's Lair by *Amerika* for Munich for ceremonies marking the anniversary of the Beer Hall Putsch in November 1923.

11 November: Hitler returned to East Prussia and resumed directing the War from the Wolf's Lair.

21 November 1941: Hitler left Wolf's Lair by *Amerika* to attend the funeral services for Luftwaffe General Udet.

28 November 1941: Hitler attended the funeral of Luftwaffe ace Werner Molders at the Air Ministry in Berlin.

29 November: Hitler returned to East Prussia and resumed directing the War from the Wolf's Lair.

2 December 1941: Hitler travelled by plane to Poltava in Russia for a conference at Army Group South.

4 December 1941: Hitler returned to East Prussia and resumed directing the War from the Wolf's Lair.

9 December 1941: Hitler leaves East Prussia by special train *Amerika* for a meeting with Grand Mufti of Jerusalem.

16 December: Hitler returned to East Prussia and resumed directing the War from the Wolf's Lair.

1942

12 February 1942: Hitler departed for Berlin for the funeral of Dr Fritz Todt who died at the Wolf's Lair in a plane crash on 8 February 1942.

15 February 1942: Hitler returnd to East Prussia and resumed directing the War from the Wolf's Lair.

15 March 1942: Hitler departed for Berlin in *Amerika* to address the *Heldengedenktag* ceremonies.

16 March 1942: Hitler returnd to East Prussia and resumed directing the War from the Wolf's Lair.

24 April 1942: Hitler departed for Berlin to the Berghof and prepare an address meeting at the Reichstag.

3 May 1942: Hitler returned to East Prussia and resumed directing the War from the Wolf's Lair.

21 May 1942: Hitler departed by special train *Amerika* to Berlin to attend the funeral of Gauleiter Rover.

24 May 1942: Hitler returned to East Prussia and resumed directing the War from the Wolf's Lair.

28 May 1942: Hitler departed by *Amerika* to Berlin to deliver a speech to officer candidates at the Sportspalast on 29 May.

31 May 1942: Hitler returned to East Prussia and resumed directing the War from the Wolf's Lair.

4 June 1942: Hitler left Wolf's Lair by aircraft for Finland and a conference with the Finnish leaders. Later that day Hitler returned to East Prussia and resumed directing the War from the Wolf's Lair.

9 June 1942: Hitler left the Wolf's Lair by *Amerika* for the funeral of SS-Obergruppenführer Heydrich who had been assassinated in Prague by British agents. Hitler then journeyed to Munich where he attended the funeral of NSKK leader Adolf Huhnlein. He then returned to the Reich Chancellery in Berlin.

26 June 1942: Hitler returned to East Prussia and resumed directing the War from the Wolf's Lair.

17 July 1942: Hitler and his entire headquarters staff left the Wolf's Lair in sixteen aircraft for Hitler's new Ukraine headquarters in Vinnitza called *Werewolf.*

31 October 1942: Hitler returned to East Prussia and resumed directing the War from the Wolf's Lair.

7 November 1942: Hitler departed from the Wolf's Lair on *Amerika* for Munich for the 9 November ceremonies.

23 November 1942: Hitler returned to East Prussia and resumed directing the War from the Wolf's Lair.

1943

16 February 1943: Hitler travelled by plane to Zaporozhye for a conference with Field Marshal von Manstein in Army Group South. Within a couple of days Hitler returned to Werewolf where he remained for four weeks.

13 March 1943: Hitler and entire headquarters staff returned to East Prussia and resumed directing the War from the Wolf's Lair.

20 March 1943: Hitler departed by special train *Brandenburg* to Berlin for the *Heldengedenktag* ceremonies. Hitler then left for the Berghof.

30 June 1943: Hitler returned to East Prussia and resumed directing the War from the Wolf's Lair.

19 July 1943: Hitler departs by aircraft to Feltre in Italy for a conference with Mussolini.

19 July 1943: Hitler returned to East Prussia later that day and resumed directing the War from the Wolf's Lair.

27 August 1943: Hitler departed from the Wolf's Lair and flew to *Werewolf* for one day to confer with Manstein.

28 August 1943: Hitler returned to East Prussia and resumed directing the War from the Wolf's Lair.

8 September 1943: Hitler departed from the Wolf's Lair and flew to Zaporozhye for one day for a conference with commanders of Army Group South.

8 September 1943: Hitler returned to East Prussia and resumed directing the War from the Wolf's Lair.

7 November 1943: Hitler departed from the Wolf's Lair aboard *Brandenburg* to Munich for the annual ceremonies.

17 November 1943: Hitler returned to East Prussia and resumed directing the War from the Wolf's Lair.

20 November 1943: Hitler departed from the Wolf's Lair by *Brandenburg* to Breslau to address the annual class of officer candidates. He then went on to Berlin and the Berghof.

22 December 1943: Hitler returned to East Prussia and resumed directing the War from the Wolf's Lair.

1944

15 March 1944: Hitler departed from the Wolf's Lair by his special train *Brandenburg* where he met with Hungarian Chief of State Horthy at Schloss Klessheim on 18 March. Hitler then journeyed to the Berghof where he and his headquarters resided until construction work at the Wolf's Lair was completed.

15 July 1944: Hitler returned to East Prussia and resumed directing the War from the Wolf's Lair.

20 July 1944: Hitler and entire headquarters staff left the Wolf's Lair aboard *Brandenburg* and moved to the headquarters to the Reich Chancellery in Berlin.

After Hitler moved to the Reich Chancellery building work still continued on the Wolf's Lair even whilst he directed the Ardennes offensive from his Western Front headquarters, *Adlerhorst*. On 15 January 1945 he returned to Berlin where he directed the War from the Reich Chancellery and then from the *Führerbunker*. Between 25 and 26 January, as the Russians advanced through East Prussia and closed in on the Wolf's Lair, Hitler finally ordered the demolition of his Eastern Front headquarters.

Appendix G

Abbreviations and Equivalent Ranks

FBB – Führer-Begleit-Bataillon (Führer Escort Battalion)

FHQ – Führerhauptquartier (Führer Headquarters)

HQ – Headquarters

NSKK – National Socialist Motor Corps

OKH – Oberkommando des Heeres (High Command of the Armed Forces)

OKW – Oberkommando der Wehrmacht (High Command of the Armed Forces; Hitler's staff as Supreme Commander)

OT – Organization Todt (Third Reich civil and military engineering group in Germany named after its founder, Fritz Todt, an engineer and senior Nazi figure who died in an aircraft crash at Rastenburg in early 1942)

RSD – Reichssicherheitsdienst (Reich Security Service)

RSHA – Reichssicherheitshauptampt (Reich Security Head Office)

SD – Sicherheitsdienst (Security Service)

SS – Schutzstaffel (Protection or Guard Detachment)

Waffen-SS – Fully militarised formations of the SS

German Army	Waffen-SS	British Army
Gemeiner, Landser	Schütze	Private
	Oberschütze	
Grenadier	Sturmmann	Lance Corporal
Obergrenadier		
Gefreiter	Rottenführer	Corporal
Obergefreiter	Unterscharführer	
Stabsgefreiter		

German Army	Waffen-SS	British Army
Unteroffizier	Scharführer	Sergeant
Unterfeldwebel	Oberscharführer	Colour Sergeant
Feldwebel		
Oberfeldwebel	Hauptscharführer	Sergeant Major
Stabsfeldwebel	Hauptbereitschaftsleiter	
Sturmscharführer		Warrant Officer
Leutnant	Untersturmführer	Second Lieutenant
Oberleutnant	Obersturmführer	First Lieutenant
Hauptmann	Hauptsturmführer	Captain
Major	Sturmbannführer	Major
Oberstleutnant	Obersturmbannführer	Lieutenant Colonel
Oberst	Standartenführer	Colonel
Oberführer		Brigadier General
Generalmajor	Brigadeführer	Major General
Generalleutnant	Gruppenführer	Lieutenant General
General	Obergruppenführer	General
Generaloberst	Oberstgruppenführer	
Generalfeldmarschall	Reichsführer-SS	

Bibliography

Author's notes on sources of documents and correspondence

The author has six volumes of research dealing with the Wolf's Lair which include hundreds of documents, microfilm and illustrations. During research a number of individual experts shared valuable information. They include Bartlomiej Zborski, Dr Czeslaw Puciato, Wilczy Szaniec, Dr Andrzei Paczkowski, Dr Richard Raiber, Dr Hans-Jurgen Kuhn, Dr Hartmut Lehmann, Professor Peter Hoffmann, Fritz T. Stol, David Irving, and my Polish and Russian translator W. Jaworski.

The following is a general outline of sources of documents used for this volume. Published works to accompany the research can be found at the end of the bibliography.

The descriptions of the Wolf's Lair are based primarily on the author's, Dr Richard Raiber's and Professor Hoffman's investigations of the installations in 1972, 1974 and 2008. Karl-Jesco von Puttkamer's statement on 5 March 1964 and his sketch of the site also helped verify certain aspects of layout. The author drew his conclusions on the general construction of *Wolfschanze* by relying partly on correspondence in 1998 and 1999 with Dr Raiber, and also his works in *After the Battle No. 19* (London 1978) and sources supplied in 1999 by the National Archives [T78, Roll 351]. The author also consulted [Führerhauptquartier Volumes] NA Record Group 242-HLB-4494a, which contain serials of 35-mm Leica contact prints of views taken by Heinrich Hoffmann at *Wolfschanze*. Sources relating to the erection of the perimeter fences and the minefield, the author consulted the NA RG 242-HB collection. The author's Polish expert Bartlomieji Zborski, US National Archives KTB FHQ mirco-copy Nr.6, the State Archives of the Russian Federation, and nine page document supplied by Dr Andrzej Packowski, who also wrote a Polish article on what the Soviet NKVD found when they entered *Wolfschanze* and surrounding area in February 1945. The descriptions of Security Zone II, are primarily drawn from published memoirs of General Walter Warlimont, deputy chief of operations for the OKW, in his book, *Inside Hitler's Headquarter 1939–1945*.

Information containing important security measures at the headquarters was obtained through the US National Archives. The *K.T.B des commandant des Führerhauptquartier*, NA RG 242, Microcopy T78, roll 351. This is the war diary of the Führer-Begleit-Bataillon, which composed of the Army and Luftwaffe which furnished perimeter security for the Wolf's Lair through material located at the Hoover Institute. Also correspondence in 1998 and 1999 with Professor Peter Hoffmann, and his book *Hitler's Personal Security*.

For Hitler's health the author used Dr Morell's diaries. In 1981, Morell's diaries were handed over to the US National Archives, which partly filmed them on T253/62. David Irving translated and annotated them, and these have been used in certain passages of this volume, and from David Irving's book, *The Secret Diaries of Adolf Hitler's Doctor*.

For the first Russian winter the author used the German Air Ministry summary dated 22 September 1941 US National Archives [T77/32/0786]. Regarding the despondency at the Wolf's Lair in late 1941, the author primarily used David Irvings's Reel 4 – Section 18 from the private letters of Frau Schmundt's (Husband Rudolf Schmundt who was Hitler's chief Wehrmacht adjutant 1938–1944). Reel 6 – Section 29. The author took typed extracts of unpublished memoirs of Nicolaus von Below, Hitler's Luftwaffe aide until April 1945. Reel 7 Section 36. Records of interviews with Frau Christa Schroder, Nicolaus von Below, and Otto Gunsche.

The author's version at the Wolf's Lair of events during the Battle for Moscow until December 1941 mainly used diaries of Bock, Halder, Hewel, and the war diaries of Army Group Centre. Other notes and sources dealing with this period were drawn from the US National Archives [NA RG 242-HLB-4494 to 7242a].

The author also used Rommel's own papers held at the US National Archives (T84/276 and 277), General Zeiteler's manuscript (N63/79 held at the Bundesarchiv in Frieburg. Written statements by members of the Stenographic Service at the Wolf's Lair, written for US authorities, were also acquired.

The author based his accounts on Hitler's move to *FHQ Anlage Wehrwolf* on 16 July 1942 from correspondence with Dr Richard Raiber, Keitel's published memoirs, and published extracts from the diary of Christa Schroder.

Material relating to Hitler's relationship with his General Staff was obtained from the published *Halder War Diary*, extracts from the private diary of Frau Anneliese Schmundt, the personal papers of Helmuth Greiner, author of the OKW war diary at the Wolf's Lair until 1943 and excerpts of Nicloaus von Below's memoirs. Written statements by members of the stenographic service at the Wolf's Lair, written for the US authorities in 1945, also helped.

General Zeitler's (N63/79) papers, and General Greiner's pocket diary on microfilm reel 5 section 25 (A) David Irving was used throughout. Various letters and manuscripts of staff at *Wolfschanze* supported many of the facts, including Frau Junge, Below, Greiner, Engel and Zeitzler. General Guderian's notes with Hitler were another vital part which included the Bundesarchiv file H16/236. Army Group B war diary was used to support claims that Hitler believed the Allies would strike at Normandy in the summer of 1944. For the War in the West the author consulted a study by Scheidt, deputy chief OKW historian documents found in the National Archives RG 407.

For the 20 July assassination attempt the author consulted a number of documents including the OKW war diary (T77/1432/0620). Stenographer Thot's diary, Schmundt's and Keitel's version of events and Peter Hoffmann's Study in his book, *Hitler's Personal Security*. In addition I researched Heinz Linge's appointment book for Hitler from October 1944 to February 1945 (T84/22). Various Hitler war conferences were consulted during the latter half of 1944.

Journals

'Wolfschanze – English Tourist Guide', Czestaw Puciato

'Die Wolfschanze', Wilczy Szaniec w Gierlozy

'Die vergessenen Führerhauptquartiere', Dr Hans-Jurgen Kuhn

Explorator, Issue No.4

After the Battle Series No.19, 'Guide to Hitler's Headquarters'

Published Sources

Buck, Gerhard, *Das Führerhauptquartier 1939–1945*, Zusammengestellt hrsg, 1979

Bullock, Alan, *Hitler and Stalin*, Harper Collins, 1992

Halder, Franz, *Halder War Diaries 1939–1942*, Greenhill Books, 1988

Hoffmann, Peter, *Hitler's Personal Security*, Macmillan Press Ltd, 1979

Irving, David, *Hitler's War*, Focal Point, 1991

Irving, David, *The Secret Diaries of Professor Morell*, Grafton, 1990

Johnson, Aaron L., *Hitler's Military Headquarters*, James Bender Publishing, 1999

Linge, Heinz, *Bis zum Untergang: Als Chef des Persönlichen Dienstes bei Hitler*, 1980

Manstein, Eric von, *Lost Victories*, Greenhill Books, 1987

Schroeder, Christa & Anton Joachimsthaler, München: Langen Müller, 1985

Seidler, Franz W. & Dieter Zeigert, *Hitler's Secret Headquarters*, Greenhill Books, 2007

Index